The Hatch

Also by Colin Browne

Poetry

* *The Properties*
* *The Shovel*
* *Ground Water*
  Abraham
  Laments of the Dying Boy
  Down the Sunline

Prose

*Motion Picture Production in British Columbia, 1898–1940:
A Brief Historical Background and Catalogue*

* Published by Talonbooks

THE HATCH

poems and conversations

Colin Browne

Talonbooks

Talonbooks
278 East First Avenue, Vancouver, British Columbia, Canada V5T 1A6
www.talonbooks.com

First printing: 2015

Typeset in Arno
Printed and bound in Canada on 100% post-consumer recycled paper

Interior and cover design by Typesmith
Illustrations by Colin Browne

Talonbooks gratefully acknowledges the financial support of the Canada Council for the Arts, the Government of Canada through the Canada Book Fund, and the Province of British Columbia through the British Columbia Arts Council and the Book Publishing Tax Credit.

Library and Archives Canada Cataloguing in Publication

Browne, Colin, 1946–, author
    The hatch / Colin Browne.

Poems.
Includes bibliographical references.
ISBN 978-0-88922-938-9 (PBK.)

    I. Title.

PS8553.R69H38 2015   C811'.54   C2015-900369-5

For Marian and Susanna

. . . a books of days

It is you again, overcoming beauty,
with a web of grief and serenity,
with the unattainable stricken thing
that our people fashioned in obscurity
out of hardship and passion,
until there came out of it the marvel

– SORLEY MACLEAN
"A Girl and Old Songs" (1970)

on the flood
      blizzards
            phytoplankton
     sifting air
from the sea

          gills sweep
      ashore, provisionally
plantigrade
      welcome home
          krill sieves!

sun strikes
      quartz
         a blaze!
      liberator
love's voice

For Tom

come in
sit down
would you like a coffee?
talk to me
i want your opinion
i need your opinion
talk to me
i want to ask you
what do you think?
what is your name?
what are you doing?
there's someone i'd like you to meet
oh talk to me
talk to me

■

my pavilion is draped with lungs
the whale's on the beach
dawn bronzes the stays

ash domes, effigies
crowd the headland –
who does not pine
for the unseen?

how beautiful the hands
that make love in dreams
like young vines

what furnishes lift?
feathers?

did i tell you i loved the Charlie Parker
in the Doug Cranmer exhibition?

existence is invisible
its quills are barbed
the little sacks
rattle the flaps

a cloud endowed with divinity
awakens the beloved
with a fragrant breeze
its "lightning-gleams
hidden deep within"

headland, where
we wait in our skins
for a sign

the long peace
is coming
undone

this picture's problem
is that it wants
to sound like what

words look like
this poem's problem
is that it thinks

it looks like what
it thinks thoughts
sound like

there are lost languages

*An Italian Fascist told the Rev. H. W. Fox of a serious
weakness in Italian life before the advent of Fascism:*
> *"What was wrong with our working people before the war
> was that they used to think and talk too much about politics.
> They were all right when they were working, for then their
> minds were on their work; they were all right when they were
> asleep, for then they didn't think at all, at least consciously.
> Their leisure hours were a danger spot for the whole nation."*

— GAETANO SALVEMINI (1936)

there are lost languages
i lament their passing
the human hive becomes coarser and
more stupid each time the phrases
of an intricate and beautiful language are silenced
my nation has rolled its sleeves up its powerful young arms
and taken a mattock to the poems
and melodies that are its sacred trust
its corporations, indemnified and indifferent to their occupation
strangle regional dialects to subsidize clichés
we're a nation of bullies
once we saluted the Union Jack
now it's the concussion,
lines of riot police
and the chill of retribution
i've been imagining the PM this weekend
in his improbable suit and toupée
barking at the big guys, spewing innuendo
bullying his G20 colleagues
hectoring and smirking as they strive
to overcome or inflate their catastrophes,
aiming with his little bully's smile
for the front row of the photograph

imperium

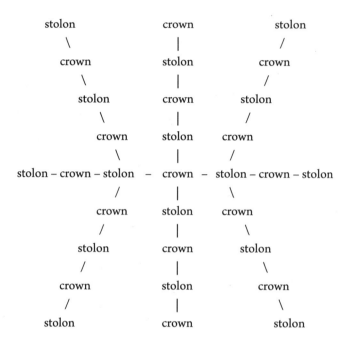

■

a whistle from
the sky

the wing bone
of a swan

ear fire

for d., on her birthday

what did   we expect?

an excursion   to tenderness?

is that why we   fled that shore?

a crow scouts

the katsura

there's a hoop   around that mask

"yes, but what   did you *hear*?"

a bird's

wing

what can a wing do?

map the sky   with a feather

sound a pibroch   on a bone

what is the eye

to an ear?

A shore, or Colin in Dogtown
(Boston to Gloucester to Boston)

"You can't win one," he said. "You've got to earn it.
      Harvard's got seventeen, the most of any school."
      I fixed on his neck.
      "It's not a contest," he said, and he began:
      "Five in the Civil War, one in the Indian Wars,"
      and on through each calamity.

What's it to us if Harold Ross scrambled after Rudolph Valentino's opera hat
      as it rolled out into the street when Valentino pitched
      to the pavement outside the Ambassador Hotel?
      The beak, the leg, in that disposition.

My friend spread his arms from one edge of the table to the other
      to illustrate the incommensurability of eternity.
      He placed his finger in the middle.
      "We're insignificant," he said, recollecting nights spent
      on the bridges of southbound seiners,
      gazing out to where the sea is not a fence
      the way my failures are a fence.

Two fingers make a shark. The bus line is Peter Pan.
      Please tell me why the big things are grey or green.

Four hundred and twenty-six Medals of Honor were issued during
      the Indian Wars that spanned three centuries from 1622 to 1924.
      When Valentino collapsed on West 45th
      men were still dying from the Indian Wars.
      Ross took the hat home thinking he'd return it
      when its owner's scalp quit the hospital.

Only she and her mother live now in the Fort Square flat
            across from Rocky Neck, the Greasy Pole
        and the salt handbag of human history.
        "On stormy nights," she says, "the whole house shakes.
        We feel the spirits of my grandparents.
        The Poet too," she says, with her perfect, white teeth.
        The house looks to have been redone, I say,
        new siding, new windows, new frames.
        "Thank you," she says.

MacLean's Hallaig girls, hailing their *"ruined homes"* on Raasay –
        a *"wood,"* he calls them:

> *"The window is nailed and boarded*
> *through which I saw the West*
> *and my love is at the Burn of Hallaig,*
> *a birch tree, and she has always been*
>
> *between Inver and Milk Hollow,*
> *here and there about Baile-chuirn:*
> *she is a birch, a hazel,*
> *a straight, slender young rowan."*

Laurence and Lorna Marshall in the Kalahari with their kids
        and their Polaroid camera in 1950 thinking,
        Nifty, eh? Pictures while
        U wait. Isn't that nifty?
        A man named /Qui was given a Polaroid
        snapshot with his likeness on it.
        "What should I do with it?" he asked,
        passing it back.

The sardines were airlifted from the Azores and slept the entire way.

D. H. Lawrence in New Mexico, 1922:

> "Never shall I forget the Indian races, when the young men, even
> the boys, run naked, smeared with white earth and stuck with
> bits of eagle fluff for the swiftness of the heavens, and the old
> men brush them with eagle feathers, to give them power. And
> they run in the strange hurling fashion of the primitive world,
> hurled forward, not making speed deliberately. And the race is
> not for victory. It is not a contest. There is no competition. It is a
> great cumulative effort. The tribe this day is adding up its male
> energy and exerting it to the utmost – for what? To get power,
> to get strength: to come, by sheer cumulative, hurling effort of
> the bodies of men, into contact with the great cosmic source of
> vitality which gives strength, power, energy to the men who can
> grasp it, energy for the zeal of attainment."

Inadvertently, I became the peristaltic or was it the periphrastic tube beneath the veranda
of William James. The first soul past the porte cochère clucked.
On the Dutch door a stencilled "ROUGE" kindled a bladder-
full of split figs adjacent to the corporation's
Forged Affidavits project.

On days like this, house sparrows have a gift for hydration.

Harold Ross, poking his pate into the office of the checking department:
"Is Moby Dick the whale or the man?"

One thousand five hundred and twenty-two Medals of Honor were minted
during the U.S. Civil War. Over half of the Medals of Honor
bestowed on Canadians issued from this slaughter.
The *o* without the *u* was already sixty.

James Laughlin dedicating *New Directions in Prose & Poetry 1940* to The Men of
the Royal Air Force:
> *"It is unlikely that any of them will ever see a copy of* New Directions,
> *or that they would be particularly interested in it if they did, but can there*
> *be much doubt that the future of free culture and of the kind of writing*
> *that* New Directions *stands for depends in great measure upon the outcome*
> *of their courageous battle?"*

Breton, surreal Eeyore, self-consciously posing his reflection
in Gotham Book Mart glass in the ectoplasmic aura
of Duchamp's tableau for *Arcane 17* with the decapitated
mannequin Brentano sent packing –
we know where this was headed . . .
Down the road from Junque & Disorderly
at the Dogtown Book Shop, a loose copy
of *Le surréalisme et la peinture* –
analogue to the battered *N* in Niantic's false first of
John Greenleaf Whittier.

A small gold coin with an angel on it turned up in my pocket that day.
André Breton, how can I trust you
when you have no ear for music?

Rodolfo Alfonso Raffaello Pierre Filibert Guglielmi di Valentina d'Antonguolla,
or Rudolph Valentino, died of pleurisy in a hospital bed.
Campbell's Funeral Church hired four actors
to impersonate a blackshirt honour guard dispatched
by a grieving Mussolini. Valentino was thirty-one.
Thinking it was her husband's, Ross's wife
chucked out the opera hat two years later.

> *"Between the Leac and Fearns*
> *the road is under mild moss*
> *and the girls in silent bands*
> *go to Clachan as in the beginning,*

and return from Clachan,
from Suisnish and the land of the living;
each one young and light-stepping,
without the heartbreak of the tale."

If I were to wake you and call you to the Dance, would we shamble and snuggle
      with new force? One is another and not another
      in our house. Stillness shapes the centre.
      See, there is mercy.

                (This too can be a shoal.)

Leon Battista Alberti, *De pictura* (1435):
      "The early painter Demetrius failed to obtain the highest praise because he was
      more devoted to representing the likeness of things than to beauty."

Freud to Jung, it's said, as the *George Washington* steamed past the Statue of Liberty in
      September 1909: "They don't realize we're bringing them the plague."

Samuel Johnson on Skye, contemplating Raasay in 1773:
      "There was perhaps never any change on national manners so
      quick, so great, and so general, as that which has operated in the
      Highlands, by the last conquest, and the subsequent laws. We
      came thither too late to see what we expected, a people of peculiar
      appearance, and a system of antiquated life. The clans retain
      little now of their original character, their ferocity of temper
      is softened, their military ardour is extinguished, their dignity
      of independence is depressed, their contempt of government
      subdued, and their reverence for their chiefs abated. Of what they
      had before the late conquest of their country, there remain only
      their language and their poverty. Their language is attacked on
      every side. Schools are erected, in which English only is taught,
      and there were lately some who thought it reasonable to refuse
      them a version of the holy scriptures, that they might have no
      monument of their mother-tongue . . . Such is the effect of the late
      regulations that a longer journey than to the Highlands must
      be taken by him whose curiosity pants for savage virtues and
      barbarous grandeur."

·The wood is dark with only bracket fungus to light the way.

> We've raised our pavilion at picturesque Dissolution Falls.
> Wisteria dispatches runners and bores like a mole
> toward the crack.

On the express to Inverness in 1977, two lady travellers peering through

> the windows at abandoned stone crofts.
> "Lonely," they exclaim, "so lonely."
> Gasps of aesthetic pleasure!

Johnson, on returning from Raasay:

> *"To hinder insurrection, by driving away the people, and to govern peaceably,*
> *by having no subjects, is an expedient that argues no great profundity of*
> *politicks . . . it affords a legislator little self-applause to consider, that where*
> *there was formerly an insurrection, there is now a wilderness."*

What MacLean saw returning: birches, hazel, rowans:

> *"a wood*
>
> *going up beside the stream"*

Gertrude and Alice on the Curtis airliner on their way to see *Four Saints*

> clutching their "Hopi Indian rabbits' feet."

In the gales a young woman in a yellow skirt hears The Poet pacing in the hall.

> A mask opens its eyes. The fox licks the bed.
> A Parisian lays out the plumed headpieces of forest people
> who are gone – and most are gone.
> A poet spoons limbs into constellations.

A pulse is more insistent than a kiss.

> But what is as good as a kiss?
> And what is not wilderness?

the fire

the past is not the barrow of your sorrow
you're its wings

lombardies, a winding drive
a failed retirement complex
with flower boxes, hops, scrubbed trilobites with tyres
you can't hose the unhappiness away
you can't pretend this was not
a hell on earth
here, at the Blything Union Workhouse
men became *subjects*

on a tip from a local woman
les Chaudières uncovered a tunnel beneath the moat
and struck at the Wehrmacht in their beds
the woman's name is forgotten
the tunnel has not been seen since
                              i'm told

"each colour is a meaning," she said

how alike are the heart's tunnels
to the waiting chambers
of Wadi Qumran

is it your impression that life
spurts out of a kind of red
jelly – a blob
with glistening veins or runners
trembling to a solar pulse?

rejoice in the invigorations
of male and female
four-legged, two-legged
finned and flippered
lunged and gilled
fingers, eyebrows
flowing one into the other
their woes in time
their joys in space
their spirits soaring
round the next bend

two guys on a bench
one with fresh red scrapes
punch marks and bullet head
yelling to a third,
"just one more, for Christ's sake"

i'm waiting for the mercy truck
to pull up at the corner
and lift its silver hatch

out on the street
without a dog
without a stick
without ever hearing your name
or your own beautiful way of
saying the world into existence

a man outside the White Lunch
peering in
that mural, he said
pointing to a bare wall
portrayed his beginnings in the sky

time begins with grief
and slowly comes to
resemble your beloved

i listen for my father's voice
below the bluffs
a head rises out of the sea
"where is your mother?"
beneath my oars

women and girls, men and boys
three generations dancing in the northern way
doing their damnedest, keeping the door open
i heard wings
i heard wings move through that house

they woke us with their
hungry, unforgettable hands
we shed our skins the night
the big leaf maple lost its leaves

we left the fire burning out there
you never know who'll need it

■

a word is not a vessel
but a bridle of
buttered leather
on a bucking river
it seems i'm its canyon
you can see the problem

buggy and infant
outside the butcher
in Welsh rain, his cheeks
streaming with blood
"Come quickly!"
"Whose child is this?"

in blown glass ·
bone chips, hairs
phytolithic blobs
plucked from saints' ashes
three scoops for
the baby Buddha

was he ever a baby?
he was a canyon
now he is a vessel
here blood
became a boy.

what the "Haida painter"
described to Boas
on the Skeena
was the birth of the
word and the thing
what he withheld
is neither

■

O flat people, rise up from your punch-outs.
I've eaten my kin; what was I thinking?
I lost my wings
on a spit.
I've got my plumage on.
I've eaten my kin.
I've toasted my wings.
My wings are toast.
I taste my wings.
Flat people, rise up from your punch-outs.
Why all this *knowing*?
I'd rather have my arms around you.
I'd rather have my wings
around you.

We are like goats tied to the butcher's stake.

   – ABDUL RAHIM KHAN to MIR HASSAN KHAN
   on the Western Front (February 7, 1917)

Root Map

A translation of the station names on the Interurban line from Vancouver to Chilliwack, circa 1938. Performed at Centre A – Vancouver International Centre for Contemporary Asian Art with composer and musician Paul Plimley on November 3, 2012, as part of the exhibition entitled *To/From BC Electric Railway 100 Years* – an exhibition celebrating the centenary of the original B.C. Electric Railway terminal building at Hastings and Carrall Streets which, for several years, was the home of Centre A. The gallery has subsequently moved to new premises on East Georgia Street.

1. A '52 pickup kicking up plumes; echolocating whale!
2. A whale that boils the pearls in an unhurried nation.
3. The nation that flattens its foretopmen with no thought for their souls.
4. Souls at sea in emotion; perhaps there's only One.
5. The One that inflates like a giant fungus, a mirage *deraciné*.
6. *Deraciné* my arse; the mirage with a steeple tip kisses a steeple tip.
7. The tip of the stick battleship rises on a ripple and bobs right.
8. The right pebble doubles up on consonants.
9. Consonants like flicked matchbooks at the Embassy Café. Liver and onions, cook's midnight whisky.
10. "*Whisky per tutti!* – but for that night on Tiananmen Square.
11. Unwashable square; defiance holds the channels.
12. Channels of water and wire and enamel. A duck's the decoy.
13. Or a decoy's hawked indulgences, modelled on the transubstantiated other.

14. The other veils itself and grins. If slavers paddle in, this is your tussock.
15. Tussock for skull, rage, for sealant leaks . . . the solar hero's stumped.
16. Stumped by a blizzard, Boy Cornwell in shorts, plucky and deferent to my demise, shell brass in mind.
17. Shelley's mind, entering the aching, unravelling heart of Keats.
18. Keats on the peaks, poet on the floes.
19. The floes below *Bonhomme, les canots* lifting on the current.
20. Skookum current, rippling *V*, raise the barrel, hush the blind.
21. Blind the cranium that hoards capillaries. I hear the tractors, my son.
22. The son's red joy whittles for sticks to peel.
23. Peel the pelt, pivot the boulders.
24. Boulders whirl; minnows spine a cuff.
25. The cuff's flipped; a hawser's on the bow.
26. The bow that spooks the deer.

27. The deer that clears the ditch, the honeysuckle wall.

28. A wall of horn recalled the kill.

29. The kill at the cove, the hole, to sit in the council of seals.

30. The seals that made the son weep.

31. Weep for consonants and blankets on the heather.

32. Heather he divined, rare and white, when he was disgraced and orbiting.

33. Orbiting bees, bees to bees, bees in the vetch to bees.

34. Bees buzzing marble; word sweat for victors, for a while.

35. A while, and a conjunction, and Oedipus.

36. Oedipus the forerunner, the finishing torch.

37. A torch, an ibex bounding away from an Iron Age tomb.

38. A tomb, a constant ache; we want our sons back. We want our sons back home.

39. Home is no hearth for discouraging words.

40. Words and noise, yoked to a star zoo.

41. The zoo looms a coat.

42. The coat stitches bulbs at the edge of a moat.

43. The moat was borrowed, the sea was sore.

44. Sore as money, craving more.

45. More's a prod, the thing's a ling.

46. The ling, I said, and lunged instead.

47. Instead? I fled. My gullet's red.

48. Red border, breast and wind and theft.

49. A theft of air, the dam at night, the teeth intent on tires.

50. The tires I told I till for starlings.

51. Starlings startle the pond in a willow pattern algorithm.

52. Is algorithm a becoming, asks Lucinda, a jay, an archive of skin?

53. A skin named the whirlwind, or broom pods, say?

54. Say the log inked the long intricate tattoo of us.

55. Us possessed, or an ancient riverbed.

56. The bed is greening, serpents angle in it.

57. Its pool makes a bladder of the you: a thing, a pelt.

58. Your pelt, your spot, the poet's tree, theophany, a windbreak.

59. Windbreak. Do two verbs equal a noun? Is it the other way around? A verb
     that's an adjective keeps you peeled.

60. Peeled, is *I* adjective or claws?

61. Claws on a fox's pup, from whom you say you unravelled at the Universal
    Change. What a night!
62. Night horse, bucking. Seed on two hooves.
63. Hooves flexed, neck twisting in the shallows.
64. All shallows eve and the orphan's footfall, Adam's malice.
65. Malice in hand, cracked pots, shard hills.
66. The hill's combustible; burning its joys, its hulls, its songs.
67. The songs of bronze and, somehow, always, the whip.
68. The whip's solemn surname riding at the wrist.
69. A wrist the churning isthmus of the universe.
70. The universe harpoons contest.
71. The contest of four in view of the two, of two in view of the four.

72. Four lives down, five to go; he's a prestidigitator, sir.
73. Sir, you must stir. Who can you trust?
74. Trust scores us bareback.
75. Bareback to the Tigris on the axes of liberty.
76. Liberty was enough, but by the fourth letter we'd let it slip away.
77. Away went the owls, the swallows, the barn as well.
78. The well's voice the vole vetoed, the footprint tracker.
79. The tracker's face in the mirror's river, the weeping on that Night.
80. Night of farewells; we lost what we desired.
81. I desired each drop when the thunderheads rose.
82. A rose's thorn, riparian resuscitation.
83. Resuscitation is vertical; you finger the tip of a canopy, an ecstasy.

84. Ecstasy or tongue, the legs sprout, spout.
85. Spout, plumed victor.
86. Victor's a prime number, lustrous, with burrs and bent feathers.
87. Feathers from gills, exquisite variations on a single origin.
88. What origin's wriggle found us swimming and glistening?
89. Glistening feet, silt flowing, silvery fish, unnamed things with legs.
90. Legs as an impediment, as language may be at the mirage of the table.
91. Table, or *mappa mundi*, gate leg to the inviolable, honey for the cold.
92. The cold whistled in, we parted the reeds with Pharoah Sanders' little
    daughter, admiring the curve of the creel.
93. A creel, a prow, and now, in boots and camouflage, I marry the pussy rushes.

rideau

with his wooden
easel, a jar
of water,
a new brush

my sweet father –
pulled under
the black current
like that copy of

Tropic of Cancer
in the canal
its white wings
gleaming

and sinking
his son
on the bridge
on his knees.

hawk-eyed Monty
invading our ranks
liked what he saw:
subjects.

>   a man adorned with feathers
>   does not believe
>   that feathers make the man
>   there is no man.

i've made room for disgrace
i've tried feathers; they get sticky
the sasquatch trousers promote boils
i considered a pair of batteries

and Marshall McLuhan ears
why not? the caramel was still stiff
and the colour of my kilt
when you think of it, almost everything

has been sliced in two, almost everything
is a cross-section, or a cross-section
of a cross-section, and *merci*
Robert Lepage for the insight.

i've boned the old syntax
the ox sprouts two horns
and mistakes submission
for forgiveness. my colleagues

have been subjects for so long
they've come to believe that
collusion with authority
while railing against authority

will imbue them with the authority
to deny having acquired authority.
i'm listening to the Peggy Lee Band's
"Floating Island" and hear

a better model for being human.
i promise i won't lie to you
without knowing that
i am lying to you

> the verb is a hole in a balaclava
> begging you to monetize an organ
> and buy an armoured Escalade
> Delaware Avenue needed Chekhov

with those unbuckled steamer trunks
and England's bravest slaying the blood-
guzzling demon foes of our Anglican
puffball-eating neighbours

i was a sourpuss in rhythm band
and later, with old S. in the chem lab
his warm hand on my shoulder, Mr. B.
in the halls with his strap

and E.D., bicycle clips on his woollen
cuffs, a jazzman, *un maquisard*
in 1959 he welcomed back de Gaulle
standing erect in the 4B classroom, belting out

"La Marseillaise" in a hail of spitballs, men
we ridiculed and admired; by then i'd heard
the whispers. under eaves daubed
with symbols, fevers seized me

unassailable alchemies pried loose
a useless melancholy
in my father's childhood attic
a few steps from the suck of black water

if you see anything wiggling

give it a good squish.

Elementary Mensuration

The object of the present work is to enable boys to acquire a
moderate knowledge of Mensuration in a reasonable time.
All difficult and useless matter has been avoided ... A few
examples are added on the application of Algebra to Geometry,
to induce the aspiring student to step out from the beaten path
of Arithmetic; for no one must consider himself proficient till
he can investigate his own methods.

— SEPTIMUS TEBAY (1868)

there's no queue. sprung from
the beaten path the Imagination
bolts from the prim snares of
Cartesian determinism into the

beguiling stamens of the unattainable.
what would make you think you're
not that dog or this twisting
minnow? everything's crystal

clear till the will blurs it, and
the concealed desire to
wound another. there will be
grudges, and the world

will not alter. what may alter
is the resolve to mask your
intentions. resolve spins
capricious scrims, weirs of

forgetting, soluble renditions
of destiny, a thicket of quotients
or a vine blooming with birds'
beaks and sober, snouted creatures

you could put your finger on
for licking, but somehow the
light rolls in again, it's firm
and you'll have found yourself

once more on *the beaten path.*
you may discover that
you're chasing your tail
or that the man you meet

is a wolf you've injured
or deceived. after all this
rigmarole you may need
your courage back

a conversation

I've been meaning to ring you, said the wolf, his tail pressed against his legs. *I wasn't happy about that last piece.*

I haven't shown a soul.

You don't say?

–

This part here. He lifted a paw and pressed it down. *What's this?*

A reasonable conclusion.

Says who? And this?

Same, in the absence of . . .

. . . of . . .

. . . a transcript . . . of what was said.

But I didn't . . .

Memory can be tricky.

Wait. Let me get this straight. If it's on a piece of paper, then that's it, that's the truth? End of conversation?

More or less.

Jesus H. Christ!

Well, let's look at how they tell it in the book.

But wait, am I expected not to believe anything you say?

As you like . . .

You missed stuff. You left stuff out.

–

You never asked me, man. I was there. I was in it. Anyway, what's it to you?

It excited me intellectually. It was an irretrievably rare example of spatial time and temporal space!

–

Look, time and space in your story are totally absent. You were infinite, and you were absolutely nothing at the same time – a slave of the libido unshackled in eternity! You unmasked the illusion of dimensionality!

My ass.

You punctured the tyranny of subjectivity! You goosed gravity! Goodbye, Descartes!
    Goodbye, God!

Who?

Exactly! Now, who's responsible for that story?

No one.

Impossible.

It's always been there . . .

−

. . . I was in it. I still am.

You make it sound like a puddle.

I don't think you want to insult me . . .

Right . . .

. . . though you're on the scrawny side . . .

Unlike her?

That was something!

Ever seen that sort of thing before?

Seems she can have only two pups to a litter.

Not necessarily.

−

The story says "curious things" have occurred in your life already. Such as . . . ?

That face. Freaked me out, man.

−

The lower face. The big one.

You liked that?

I believe it's the first time one of your women ever showed herself to us.

Surprised?

I thought it was a ghost.

And the man?

He just stood there, watching. He was twenty paces away. I could smell his liver.

But you . . . ?

No.

Were you embarrassed.

I think they were in search of a little . . . what do you call it?

Hanky-panky?

You pink sticks are something else. Everything's a euphemism with you!

How about him? Do you think she would have shown herself to him?

He covered his eyes.

What happened next?

You said there was no next.

—

A blizzard entered my brain.

And?

They were gone.

And you?

Where could I go? I couldn't go home. I dug a hole in the snow and slept there.

And?

I haven't been home since.

Your family?

On its own.

And now?

Now? You torment me with what I no longer know.

my knees

pistons
in a two-stroke

a man pitches headfirst
off a picnic table
into the grass
where his comrades lie smoking
and opening beer
americas tumble with him

a son lies on a
bench, his boils
burn in the sun
torn from their doorsteps
these men seek
refuge, trees for their birds

my grandfather steps
off the platform
into God's Country
God the demolisher
it's said no one saw
the rind, but how

could anyone miss it?
he returned to his log
cabin carrying the false tooth
with the bead of cyanide
for the day compromise
proved intolerable

my knees

pestles
in an ossuary

■

forget the rubber paddles of the sullen shale the louche hills and
Costco vales that curdle vials of Ayurvedic spit or toss off
panoramas of Khobani flossing downhill pending lank incisors into
manifestations of mock amphibians gripping the lens of antiquity or
ventriloquy as contrails above warlords in mid-sniff crouching in the
toxic stains and tree splinters of our fathers she really did not believe
her peepers or the iridescent Houdini extensions and compressions
of shrikes' necks while angling wagered by the dismaying invocations
of a professional mandrake's penny in a beaver hat forgetting his
Georgics at the lacy precipice of an infant's polyamorous bacchanal
in the little basket or wedding blouse that retaliated with sculpins and
tubed Hudson's Bay cream against the clawed vetch waterboarding
the ancestral gravy boats and spectral botchers into whose axe-wash
we make a brief, spastic splash, apparently to breed while absorbed in
enticing interrogations of propulsive lip-flap on said splenetic rocks
the ladies stare as a crazed pinch-hitter scrawls on a tree parasite,
grimaces, wails, and romances the tide from the pinched stern and
dares to whisper the *name* when the chiton's speared in the lobby of
the oceanic gratitudes i've poached your lewd drawers with dude
roars on loud doors slamming into ice, or the gargle that excites a
tremor on the inner wire as if a flicker's tail is stilling a cedar quiver
forget the rubber paddles of the sullen shale the louche hills and

swan

(FOR C.W.)

dit dit dit   dit da da   dit da   da dit

dit dit dit   dit da da   dit da   da dit

dit dit dit   dit da da   dit da   da dit

rending night from day

O swan

tearing day from speckled night

dit da da dit   dit da da dit   dit da da dit   dit da da dit

you are standing into danger

dit dit da   dit dit da   dit dit da   dit dit da

your lights are out, or burning badly

dit dit dit   dit da da   dit da   da dit

dit dit dit   dit da da   dit da   da dit

da da da   da da da   da da da   da da da

man overboard!   man overboard!

da dit da   da dit da   da dit da   da dit da

da da da   da da da   da da da   da da da

you should stop your vessel instantly

da da da   dit dit dit   dit da da   dit da   da dit

night rent from day

da dit dit   da dit dit   da dit dit   da dit dit

it is not for herself she grieves

da da dit   da da dit   da da dit   da da dit

but for the one she could not save

O swan   swan

dit   dit   dit   dit

i am directing my course to starboard

dit dit   dit dit   dit dit   dit dit

i am directing my course to port

oh, swan   swan   oh, swan

my darling swan

dit da dit da dit   dit da dit da dit

dit da dit da dit   dit da dit da dit

granny soot

i strung fence for the verb
like a stumped squire
with egg boxes in the barn
bars of Sunlight in the sink
hens got in and pecked at
and a glory of a civilization
next door about which
i was indifferent

i loved a British drunk
and made believe he wasn't
i dreamed he was my dad
as if a decaying alcoholic in an English grave
was an improvement
over the kind, conflicted man
living up the hill with
his safety on

a lick of the century's cranks
undid the id in a head
i thought was mine – a sparkler
in a dim room of
its own devising
certain that any thing in
the universe that was not it
shared no existence with it

and had no call on existence at all
with god splinters it tanned
an engine of bone
and a zealot's cortex
in the mothering shadow
of a sacred hill
but a round of wood
in the woodshed was

itself and nothing else
i was an open mouth
without feathers or fins
a nestling at the sign
of the celestial bear
i got a hook in the head
of the weir i wove
in the trickle of a shallow

ditch where starlings wheeled
drunk and shrieking over
Garry oaks, seeding Eden
in the shed where the head
tabled scores at night
with a single egg-inducing
incandescent light
i was a moon, a bachelor

whistling at termites
the bust is a bust (as a bust is not)
or a bull's eye daubed red
for assassins
bulls forget (unlike hooks)
things crumple, the beautiful
productions of the spirit
are sawn to powder

each fall the cottonwoods
die a little then return
in a storm of soft seed
along the river
"Comrade!" cries
a passing head
"Have you seen my love?
I am undone."

Keaton once told me that he and Chaplin missed the sound of the cameras cranking after they stopped making silent films. Because of the rhythm.

– PENELOPE GILLIATT (1974)

a surgeon

off the night boat, bored
to tears with himself

steps onto the wharf
in Victoria

expecting cops
what the hell

he'd come clean, he *is* one
who'd not be

in this cesspool of
hand-wringers

bloodsuckers, and
the physicians who

keep them breathing to
profit from their decay?

it's august first
the grass is dry

the light is pale and flat
ten months from now

the Consul will lend
Jacques Laruelle

a volume that will fall
open to the concluding

words of Marlowe's
Doctor Faustus:

*"Terminat hora diem;
terminat auctor opus."*

"Who *do* you serve?"
he asks the driver

who because there is
no other direction

speeds north, "What makes
you bite your tongue," he asks

"What knowledge do you suppress
in order to lubricate

the mass hallucination
of the state?"

I'm funnel number four
he thinks, opening a window

trees part for a lake
commemorating

a 36-gun Royal Navy
man-of-war propelled

by twenty-five thousand
square feet of canvas

dispatched halfway
around the world

to terrorize those
who refused

to be enslaved –
"viri a diis recentes . . . "

arbutus gives way
to cedar and fir

spruce travels east now
on both lines

for fuselages, and steel for
rivets in warships

on the ways in
Birkenhead yard

where silver slippers in
a great hall become

boots in a nameless
face and an infant is

singed and dipped to confer
inheritance and immortality

before God, which may
just be the problem

on this August morning
beneath the Malahat

he can saw a man apart
and stitch him back

together, but men
are dying

and he's as insufferable
as a Hemingway hero

that's a pipsqueak
way to go, it is not

wrong to want to do great
things, to be alive

the car pulls into
a parking lot

he opens the door
to the sky where it

grazes the earth
the comrade within

seizes hold of his ribs
and lifts him

out of his cage . . .
. . . not yet

he is not done yet
there's an island

and a rental outfit
on the beach

he pays the kid
and leaves a tip

he tells the driver
come when i call you

off with his shoes, socks
his keel cuts a notch

the bow swings west
he ships oars

the hatch

in these borrowed breeks this chemise that vest and tail lamp a dawn of glimmering
bronze what is this beast's D9 to glory? forward-bending knees?

ear porous? for us? he was gone but on his bedroom table we found the book and
white freesias.

a trout rising to wed the fly.

a sharp-shinned hawk rising with a field mouse, its legs still running.

my father with his silver monogrammed hairbrush absent rows of bristles.

within their categories i'll make mine a wren's egg.

at the Embassy Café with a tumbler of whisky on the tabletop the cook staring
at the floor.

Éluard, 1939, his red chest swollen have you seen the ghost on the sixth floor?
Man Ray was done by then.

Finkielkraut: "We have not learned to be wary of the beatific smile of fraternity."

in the pink Hank Snow in pink a Guysborough guy his guys in jade.

in the salmon house order is the pursuit of harmony still it's nice to put your feet up
and get the skins off.

when Eddie Hubbard crashed into the Inner Harbour in 1919 the B-1 went south
for repairs.

the morning he brought her down in Brentwood Bay my grandmother rowed her
daughters out to touch it you'll never see another one she said it was her
farewell to the brief, unpleasant experiment with Modernity.

Adorno on music: "It has always been a protest, however ineffectual, against myth,
against a fate which was always the same . . ."

Wilson Duff in the collection forty-five years ago, an argillite cockle in his palm,
unaware that M. was watching, or so she thought. Mankind was released
from this shell, he said, we clambered out of a cockle just like this . . . and
Charlie Endenshaw carved it shut.

at Douglas Lake – Spaxomin – a breeding pair, in 1951, planting the flag; ospreys turn
above them, observing the habits of trout.

the lava field

or without
in the lava fiexld

sicxk of himself
on the nigxht boat

this smallpox takes
the piss out of proxfits

wisdom teeth, then cervix
then the armisxtice

when I lisxten it's
we're safer, not safe

leaves bore legs
wind adores

across the on the
in the dowxn the

bring your shovel
and a strong knixfe

takes a bite
out of

wires, wirxed corners
who's counting

it's Rudolph that
goes down in hisxtory

de Montaigne on cannibals
a sweextness

tunnel leggers
not craxftsmen

but specixalists
all the same

I do not want to be forced to put on the glove of a skeleton that has been extracted from an anatomy of the false cosmos.

– ANTONIN ARTAUD (1947)

■

she said, may i ask
you something?
what if i crossing the border
into my country
and they don't let me in?

       they escort you across the road,
       the bus driver said

            a man behind me was weeping
            in his mother's arms

       the next bus, he said

       will send you back

but how is it that
in Canada, my country
they are so hard
to let me in . . . ?

       you hide your words, he said,
       say nothing

but i'm now the daughter citizen
have they not
to let me in . . . ?

            son and mother in the glaring
            interrogation room

where else can i go
she said,
what kind of border is this
where you are afraid
that you will not be
allowed home?

the drones, Helen tells me
launched themselves
from a crack in the walk
this morning

in the desert men
stoop to lift
meteor specks
off the hot sand

from fire to ice to fire
to a Middle Kingdom
clavicle
Fe Co Ni

carnelian, lapis lazuli
pixellating wings
solar spasm
cargo from the stars

■

in the oak grove
an old serpent
stirs

it's 1913
the British Board
of Film Censors

has pre-empted
its masters' dismay
by chopping out

a few frames
from a potboiler
"calculated to *demoralize*

the public." oh dear
the ship of state
has sprung a leak

the ineptly concealed
stands revealed
the pox is

in the barracks
the fox is
in the sheets

the indifference
that masks the
masters' contempt

for the common man
(whom they'd prefer
to euthanize)

risks exposure, and
a daughter's virtue
is no small thing.

"Summon the poets!
Poodle up, gents
do something

with that moon
of yours. Rouse
the decent

working man
to action!"
"Take that,

spiritual pus!"
indignation
consumes a man

from within; thus
would a double
snare be laid.

the scaly one
eases his coils.
with the kiss

of a truncheon
or a lick of
the whip, a foreigner

or a degenerate
will be hauled in,
victory declared

fresh doggerel will
soon propel the
unfortunate virgins

to France or somewhere
there'll be no more talk
of *demoralization.*

■

the lamp is burning
a book has fallen over
my neck is bent
click!
in the darkness
a hatch

drunken wings

who are you?

■

they wanted us to be
a new them
a them not doomed

all they brought
was doom

ERRATA

Page 62, 10th line from bottom. **he did not notice** should read **he did notice**

Page 95, line 2. **complete** should read **complex.**

Page 117, 2nd line from bottom. **Throughout this swarming period, etc.** should read: **At the beginning of this swarming period, the larvae are few and small; at the end they are few and large. For the greater part of the time they are abundant and there is**

Page 134, line 3. **eggs of Woods Holl** should read **eggs at Woods Holl**

– THE CANADIAN OYSTER (Jos. Stafford, 1913)
Notice tipped in after original printing

Intoxicated by the heady wine of newly acquired power,
fearsome like wild animals who see no difference between good
and evil, slaves to women, insane in their lust, drenched in
alcohol from head to foot, without any norms of ritual conduct,
unclean . . . dependent on material things, grabbing other
people's land and wealth by hook or crook . . . the body their
self, its appetites their only concern – such is the image of the
western demon in Indian eyes.

– SWAMI VIVEKANANDA (1863–1902)

■

Cendrars, in 1912
on the proofs of
the new edition
of *Le Transsibérien*
for les Éditions des
Hommes Nouveaux
striking *bordel*
scribbling *hôtel*

Oedipus, groping from rock to oak

Césaire: *"I am talking about*
those who, as I write this,
 are digging the harbour
of Abidjan by hand.
I am talking about millions of men
torn from their gods,
their land, their habits,
their life – from life,
from the dance, from wisdom."

a forest, a pit, the sea

here, among these birches
you'll ~~likely~~ find the evidence
you seek

Haiti

poète et *prince*
in Port-au-Prince
lecturing at the Rex, his tail
                    a lit fuse
then Malcolm, a mess
                    a wilderness
on the SS *Donald Wright*
bound for
            Manhattan
                "Frère Jacques"
                "Frère Jacques"

Henri Lefebvre, years later, in conversation with himself, on Lowry:
        "he almost manages
        to bring beauty
        back to life again"

heel beel
big *wheel*
sea weed
wool *coat*
*butter*cup
tow *rope*
log boom

a fouled image
Foul Bay
at four years old
a man in a Cowichan vest
with a black hole
through his cheek
that winter, winching
wood off the beach

a mother with her ink well
an infant with his plume
he is a stranger to me
she seems to say

■

a square of light
high up
on the hospital tower
i pedal by

Cendrars's right hand
and the arm
                    rising
in the night sky
as Orion
                    (Jeffers's *"cloud of men's palms"*

so quickly
so cruelly
my brother

so far from Montmartre

now when i dial the stars
our *grande ourse* –
Desnos's bear –
is at the switchboard
good hands you're in

                              (she spoke of *star people* and all the other
                                                        colours
                                            of the sky

■

twenty-two thousand seabirds

eighty-three thousand eggs

one hundred and eighty well-fed souls

Hirta, St. Kilda, in one year, 1697

"Everything smells of feathers."

the story i cling to:
"here's how it all began . . ."

intoxication.

form

what gives with
beauty's nose

for dismembering
and spite?

when he sang, magnolias
keeled over

stones sought stones
to roll against

the limbs of meadows
arched heavily

"Coxswain, my coxswain
in the dory of my flesh!"

when grief struck
wheat wept

birds plucked out
their tails

he grew a trunk, a sycamore
they say

young men sighed
in that shade

he laid down his lyre
and his vanity

the old gods
fumed when

he gave them
the finger

he made his home
in the reeds

among swallows, where
the moon erases

and rewrites its poem
each night

the assault
was swift

and deliberate
limbs shorn off

tossed into
the river, his

head pierced
often

and set adrift
in waves of

lamentation
the mayflower

in his mouth
and mine

Then I took a mistress, and she bore me a son, who grew up to look like a slice of the moon.

— THE ARABIAN NIGHTS

■

Buffy Sainte-Marie
in the basement
ironing her school uniform
to Carl Perkins

■

Sandy at the kitchen
table on that last
sunny morning
letting it come
into him:
"O love of my heart . . ."

■

what was waiting for me at dawn?

a sentence in the shape of a spoon

■

what we call
the Modern is
their inverted ruin
a god's head
lightly worn

oh my fathers
my scavengers
Boas
Freud
Lévi-Strauss
Breton
bull and swan
beak and womb

nesting
in others'
shapes

pegs are holes

Klee Wyck

First we must study how colonization works to decivilize the colonizer...

– AIMÉ CÉSAIRE (1955)

Emily Carr in France being told (off): "Your silent Indian will teach you more than all
    the art jargon..."
        and coming home, sailing north, and in her own words,
        begging "the Parson" to spare the lives of Louise's sons in Old Massett,
        her *"NO"* to his incubator of contagion, the Indian Industrial School, a nest of
            evangelical militancy,
        to his aggressive manner, his threats,
        to the theft of children from their own warm beds,
        to their humiliation and loneliness,
        to the beatings, the inedible rations, the abuse of trust,
        to tenderness withheld,
        to the betrayal of the Divine,
        to a nation that turned a blind eye, and its poets who for a hundred years
            cultivated ignorance,
        to the Sunday school collection boxes that bankrolled the terror,
        to the editor who after Carr's death censored 2,300 words from the Canadian
            Classics edition of *Klee Wyck,* including her defiant *"NO,"* for fear of
            alienating the churches, this in the shadow of Nuremberg,
        to the men and women who used the strap and monitored the hallways, to
            the doctors and nurses who attended to the fevers and the bruises
            and who were called in early in the morning, to those who made
            deliveries, to the ones who lived next door and saw nothing, to those
            who fear to come forward now, or who see no need to –
    as sorry a record of civic courage as you'll see anywhere.

I think you should certainly proceed with the experimental work on gas bombs, especially mustard gas, which would inflict punishment on recalcitrant natives without inflicting grave injury on them . . . I am strongly in favour of using poisoned gas against uncivilised tribes.

– WINSTON CHURCHILL (1920)

sanctuaries

1.

thinning campanula
by the front gate

startling roots
with sunlight

then, yanked up
in a clump

a lens from a pair
of spectacles

cradling ancient
light

magnifier, corm
rider

trouvaille, something
between us

we are so
hungry

2.

In the *Masjid al-Aqsa*
the noble *sanctuary*

a guide drew me
into the shade

below the wall.
"Walk here,"

he said. We did so.
"This truce,"

he said, "if it fails,
I'll fight.

That's it."
He took me

to the old gate.
O tufted night,

have you seen
my beloved?

rock wall
arsenal

3.
the nest we stuck in the cedar last year
needs sticks. it stinks.
that cherry on third was best
nice cover, nutty blossoms
open in the middle
good sticks
i liked the blue string you wove in.

4.

the *miraculous* pours
out of everything

what once drew
gasps of wonder

out of the human tube
endures

in the churn
rushing up

from the planet's core
to pool under

the Bear Mother
high above this

starry mountain saddle
roar, skookum flow

in this heart-bursting
ode soaked lee

O gush, O scree
forgive me

when i stray
from wonder

5.

"Trees hold us all together."

6.

it was, i think
your body
you were
talking about

did i tell you
that it is
the measure
of the sky?

O *lake of blood*
it is a jade
funnel
to the sky

and the soft hills
the sea, these
are things
inscribed

by you, on you
your arm is
a granite headland
seething with lichens

your hand, heart's
weir – recalling
the poet's hand
threaded through

a constellation –
reaches down tenderly
to grasp
its own fingers

reaching up . . .
"My beloveds," it exclaims
*"how we've pined
for you."*

arm, sky, lake, hand
now one

7.

what men are doing around the world:
cutting lengths of
fine chicken wire
with tin snips
folding and
stuffing them
into cracks

8.
the scent of tansy
thickens the afternoon

with carnal stirrings
above the ponds

at Jericho
my ghosts couple

in gusts, with
halyards ringing

red wings
azure sky

the wind snaps
with lightning

i ride over the bones
shouting for joy

pemberton valley

they checked in
before lunch
snow then rain

fell, as it does
in early March
a logging truck

geared down
as Jack, George
and Allan in

jackets, ties
and brogues
took a stroll

to the Co-op store
scavengers of the
unguarded gesture

picture the Earp
brothers and
Doc Holliday

without Wyatt
we're looking for
one white family

one Indian
follow them
see what . . .

yup . . . horse race
anyone you can think
of we should . . . ?

night falls early
in the mountains
the hotel dozes

except for the
beer parlour and
a couple of men

in the dining room
icing pork chops
with tinned

applesauce
by the window
Allan's enthusiastic

about Roberto
Rossellini, George
is making notes

Jack's calibrating
the sun's angle
in May

pork chops, gravy
their thumbs
and fingers form

wrinkled screens
it's montage, collage
Eisenstein and metonym

how'd Flaherty
frame that kid?
the chops show up

Allan rises to ask
the two men next
door for the

pepper and salt
one looks up
and ever so slowly

slides the shakers
out of Allan's reach
"Fuck off," he says.

For a man taking stock of himself, there can be no more valuable and far-reaching hope than in the beat of a wing.

– ANDRÉ BRETON (1944)

the pole out
back's a bird
Jerusalem

its aluminium lid
flatters any
flicker's id

see that beak
at the peak?
the drummer's

toasting his belly
on the tin
she's halfway

down, stiff-tailed
tearing off
long splinters

sparrows collect
as she digs
and pecks

a grub's pried out
they pounce
she hammers on

last week
a male pileated
flew in

and drove his beak
into the old
pole's wound

scored a line
of glistening
larvae

and zoomed off
to the northeast
that pole's got

a reputation
the drummer drums
and scans the sky

if the hawk's
watching
he won't know it

■

if you could peer
four feet through

the moraine
below the scrub

to the chrome
choke knobs

and shiny door
handles of

old chassis
filled to their

unrolled windows
with shit

pumped in through
firehoses

you'd appreciate
the cunning

of your wily
neighbours

four men

step into a car at midnight
au fin de la Section d'Or

and set out in something
like a hurricane

to colonize the deep
ruts of the

Jura-Paris road
in Francis Picabia's

Peugeot: *"une machine
à 5 coeurs"*

with the chauffeur
jammed into

the open back seat like
a bracket fungus

and Picabia gunning it
through the pass

to fetch his wife
Gabrielle Buffet

at her mother's home
in Étival, known to

locals as *La Zone*
the wings are torn off

their words in the wind
but why is the wily

chocolate grinder here?
he loves Gabrielle

he's told her so
now he raps at

her mother's door
in a gale, his ardour

newly grafted onto
an erotic tableau

involving a headlight beam
and the Jura-Paris road

meteorologies have
seduced him

the monsoon monsoons
lawns are mirrors

housebound, they
dash out for firewood

and play games
Maman encourages

Apollinaire to read
his recent poem

after a round of jack-
straws he unfolds

the opening lines
of an untitled text:

"A la fin tu es las
de ce monde ancien . . ."

on the way back to Paris
in the crowded Peugeot

Duchamp feels poorly
and arriving home

composes two pages of
alchemical notes

in which the five hearts
give birth to a headlight

who becomes
"l'enfant-Dieu,

rappelant assez le Jésus
des primitifs . . .

l'epanouissement divin
de cette machine-mère."

the child, he muses
"could . . . be a comet,

which would have its
tail in front, this tail

being an appendage of the
headlight child appendage

which absorbs by crushing
(gold dust, graphically)

this Jura-Paris road."
a little god,

his son, the comet boy
the appendage of

the appendage, and of
the Jura-Paris road

and that's it, the man
who painted *The Passage*

from Virgin to Bride
announces that

he's no longer
"the artist"

admiring the curves
on a propeller

at *le Salon de la locomotion
aérienne*

he confronts Léger
and Brancusi:

"Painting is finished. Who
could improve on

that propeller? Tell me,
can you do that?"

alloy

picture them at war's
end, she's the one

with the camera
hair like cornsilk

at midday
and the shoulders

i'd cling to
in the tub

for dear
life

he's in aviator glasses
on the rustic porch

of a Laurentian auberge
here's the snapshot

she kept when
she tossed out

the Eaton's bag
with his slides in it

including "Down a Road"
a family favourite,

a study, in fall
colours, of

the futility of longing
my father stares back

from a deck chair
here's a later one

with his son
in his arms

the consequence of
that May weekend

i picture them
two strangers

his wagging tool
his grin –

i'm in that
body now –

in retrospect
i wish for those two

sweet tenderness
and everything

working beautifully
in bed, everything

working beautifully
il y a soixante-huit ans

■

at Tent Island
a while back

Curly was jigging
for cod when

he heard the
dragging sound

of an unfamiliar
creature moving

across arbutus
leaves

he couldn't
make it out

this hunter who when
he was twelve

could hear a fawn's
heartbeat

at forty yards, then
sure enough

it showed itself
an octopus

making its way
out of the trees

across the beach
into the sea.

i saw it with my
own eyes, he said

rubbing them.
on the wharf

a few days later
he got around to

asking some of the
old Indians, he said

and they told him
and he repeated

the phrase twice:
"it was not uncommon"

they said to find one
in the bush

chewing on
arbutus bark.

watch it, Curly's
landing a big one

said my sister.
i don't really

believe it myself
said Curly

taking a mouthful
of fish

but i don't know
he said

might be it's
for the ink.

the lane

In the vast colony of our being . . .

— FERNANDO PESSOA (1932)

wolverine
in my blood

salt chuck
in my nose

plant me, when
i'm done

with the
Nootka rose

❀

in the year that
Pellegrino Turri

perfected a writing
machine for his

sweetheart – with
carbon-paper kisses

twenty-two souls
gathered on deck

in a warm wind
to pray before

the fresh graves of
New Arkhangel

as the brig
Sv. Nikolai

weighed anchor
and eased through

hostile camps and
bull kelp

[103]

into the North Pacific
bound for the last

great sea otter herd
in the world

Navigator Nikolai
Bulygin's orders:

to seize Oregon
and California

in the year of Blake's
The Last Judgement

❁

last night in the lane
a man with

a coughing dog
told me he'd seen

the light, what about
Nikola Tesla

he said, we're being held
to ransom

by that bloodsucker
Thomas Edison

was i on to Edison?
the dog peed

i'm getting a real education
he told me, online

i never went to school
past grade nine

he said, and now
fucken hell

this is scary shit
mark my words

i thought of the jar of
Serbian rosehip

jam in the fridge,
Bulygin's wife

Anna Petrovna
in their narrow cabin

the riggers and cooks
the Aleut hunters

and their wives
for whom

this was a reprieve
from hacking

seals to death on
slick, wet rocks

and collecting their
penises for Canton –

the Company guts
the colony

and the Crown
turns its head

discipline aboard
the *Sv. Nikolai*

flows from the supercargo
Tarakanov

to the poachers
and chancers

heading south with
a stout wind

in the old romance
Anna's blue eyed

and flaxen haired
the soul of Slavic

honour, a jewel in the
Imperial kedgeree

what does a captain's wife
do all day?

weeks later, near what
is called La Push

unable to clear the shore
the ship is blown

onto the beach
Anna, we're told

is the first immigrant
woman

to step ashore in
New Albion

to the Quileute, watching
from the trees

as they drag their cannons
up the beach

the strangers seem
like men possessed

they call them *ho'kwat* –
"wanderers"

madmen, who've turned
their backs

on their people
to forage in

another's forest
feuding, smelling

like shit, wallowing in
humiliation

bringing shame
on their people

still, they'd fetch
a decent price

ransom value per *ho'kwat* in 1808:
"5 patterned blankets,

5 sazhens of woollen
cloth, a locksmith's

file, 2 steel knives
1 mirror, 5 packets

of gunpowder, and the
same of small shot"

the dog begins
to wheeze

within ten years, he says
the White House

will dispatch deadly
military robots

to attack civilians
in their homes

as for who should
bear arms

he says he gets it now
i spill the bones

and peels from
the pail into

the recycling bin
his online masters

are bent on normalizing
a pre-emptive

takedown of
the state

the dog leans
its chin on

its master's thigh
(not many walks

left in those old legs)
i listen, but

there's a rage
blowing up in me

i want to shake
this gullible tool

though who's more gullible
or more of a tool

is up for grabs
the state is like

a beehive burner
hurling sparks

into the starry night
glistening bodies

toil at hatches
one morning

nothing matches
the safe is open

the cash is gone
the gate is locked

the fire is out, the
guards are armed

the state has moved on
my ancestors stole

what they could
i'm still on the take

to possess is to dispossess
and when i'm not

here, i'm still here
that's possession

❁

Philip Glass, last night:
"musicians, writers

and dancers have one foot
in the world we see

the other in the world
we can't see;

i'm in that one most of
the time," he said

when we
were rubbery

we took our pleasure
in the green salal

in the world we could
touch and see

what was marriage to
Anna and Nikolai?

tenderness? a contract?
one who'll pray

for your soul when
you're beneath a mound

on a foreign shore?
disputes rent

the *ho'kwat*. Makah
and Quileute

seized them one by one
for slaves. The Makah

captured Anna
she surfaced

months later with her
protector, a *toyon*

named Yutramaki
in a frock coat

to beg for the life of
a captured kinsman

Bulygin beseeched
her to return

she refused, he swore
to kill her

"I do not fear death," she's
said to have said

he followed her
to Kunishat

where both were met
with great courtesy

but kindness gave way
to utility

and, anyway, nothing is
ever what it seems

Anna was not a fair-haired
Russian angel

but a Creole girl
from New Arkhangel

Yutramaki they say
was the son of

John McKay, an Irish
surgeon's mate

aboard the *Captain Cook*
out of Bombay

the first military robot
to winter over

at Yuquot
put ashore

to charm his hosts
and corner the trade

for the coming season
he predictably

failed to see what
cannot be seen

they spared him
and kept him

in a far cove, stripped
of clothing

delirious with fever, chewing
on herrings' heads

he begged the first ship
he saw for mercy

it was 1787, there were
fortunes to be made

in sea otters
the slaughter

resumed, the piercing
and skinning

the ocean greasy
with offal

and a shameful silence
at slack tide

take my hand, let us
switch skins

with our fellow
creatures

so that we might know
their suffering

and honour them
rejoicing in

the exuberance
of their forms

in this way
may we learn

to honour and
adore our own

and to love
more bravely

❀

when the sharp-shinned
hawk appears

the holly tree
goes silent

the next morning
in the lane

i'll find a ring of
grey pinfeathers

aching for recurrence, pattern
(as in *father*, probably)

i careen between
a consciousness

that possesses the world
by shrinking it

into a likeness
of myself

and craving
dissolution

in the luminous
immensities

i depend on
the invisible

what would it take
to melt

into the *Via Lactea*
at Effie's Point

in late August
with birds

rustling in
arbutus trees

beneath the boulevards
of the Milky Way

and the ocean blazing
with *noctiluca* light?

old equivalences
have collapsed

the terrified
roam the lanes

drop down from your dormer
to the sidewalk

we're drilling holes
for bees

building nesting boxes
for songbirds

in the shadow
of the fig

our neighbour says
she's seen no swallows

for two years
on summer nights

beneath the Mays
our street was

once a swallow's
Champs-Élysées

now a man with a dog
in late October

on the inconsequential
edge of an anxious

nation hollowing itself out
for the lowest bidder

debates with a neighbour
swinging an empty pail

the case for armed insurrection
pinch me, wolverine

you hunk of bad news
and good news in

one nicked hide, what have
you been rolling in?

what have you got to
say for yourself?

imagine this beginning:
six naked boys

step forward with fulmar
beaks tied to their lips

❁

that winter the slaves were
handed from one master

to another, Anna Petrovna
died alone, we're told

possibly by her own hand
what of her remains?

Bulygin lost consciousness
coughing up blood

the supercargo taught his master
to master a kite

in Florence a machine
harnessed a horse

to a lover's
smudges

backed into a corner
the fulmar heaves

its guts out onto
the rocks

and with its reeking puke
restores the first light

of the first day
to the world

our flesh is not our own
nor are our bones ours

generations swim through us
we draw them

into lungs that cradle us
as we're consumed

so what have i been
clinging to?

i'd know it
if i saw it

with icicles in the garden
Jupiter in the sky

and news of insurrections
exploited

to suppress dissent and
enhance privilege

we've come to hear Benjamin
Britten's string quartets

in a jazz club priced
out of its lease

the opening chord
of the First

pries a scream
from the air

Nanking, Guernica
Madrid

the Second observes
a sacred trust:

to witness, to give
testimony

in July 1945 Britten
with Yehudi Menuhin

toured extermination camps
in Europe, playing

duets in frigid
mess halls

Bergen-Belsen
he said

there were others
perhaps Dachau

twenty-five minutes
from where i sit

at the breakfast table
this morning

the Third took wing
in Venice

in a wheelchair
near death:

restless, spectral –
evaporating

into pure light
where the sky

dissolves into
the sea

child and mother
as one

❁

to listen, to weep
to wake from

weeping, or
laughing

or making love
or holding

my child, or when
i hear my father's voice

as if he's present
here, beside me

a nation
of bones

of sparks spinning
skyward

Anna, Nikolai
Yutramaki, Tarakanov

hostages, abductors
Britten, Turri, Glass

the sleeper
in the lane

reporting for duty
to the dark web

how are they
not me?

wolverine, my captain
you know my ways

we're many in one
our hides are

live embers
this shin a flute

this scalp a shell
these gills fists

this form that
never rests

if you're a butterfly
when you find me

my name will be
Nootka rose

Qu'y puis-je?
Il faut bien commencer.
Commencer quoi?
La seule chose du monde qu'il vaille la peine de commencer.
La Fin du monde, *parbleu!*

— AIMÉ CÉSAIRE (1939)

May 25, 2014

We are sitting outside, above the sea. It's a warm late afternoon, and on our left, below us, as if she'd issued from the lower part of the house, from around the corner, my mother appears, physically fit, not bent, perhaps herself at forty, or fifty, with a nice figure, stark naked, walking past some tall shrubs to the beach. I only see her from the back. She walks confidently, on a path, I imagine, without looking back, and we do not say anything. I do not say anything. She knows where she's going, and she seems to be confident in what she's doing. When she emerges from behind the shrubs she seems to have a towel with her and she wraps it around herself as she walks down the beach to the water's edge. It seems that there are other people and kids on the sunny beach.

Reaching the water, she slips out of the towel and walks into the sea. As soon as she's deep enough, she begins swimming out. Still she does not look back, although I now think she knows that we're here, watching, otherwise she might have glanced back. She swims.

Leading out from the beach are a series of rocky islets surrounded by water when the tide is high. She swims toward one of them and appears to rest, or pause, holding on to the rock for a bit. I see her hair. It's still blonde, and the sunlight is on her shoulders and shoulder blades. She appears to lean into the rock gently, always with her back to us. There is no urgency. She does not glance or look back. Then, do I turn away for a moment? I look out and I can't see her anymore. She has gone.

The poet's room (Anna Akhmatova)

The old maple looks into the window.
And foreseeing our parting,
It extends its black and withered hand
To me as if to help.

"A POEM WITHOUT A HERO" (1942)

The poet's room is like any other room –
a divan that doubles as a bed, shelves
of books, a desk, chests stuffed with paper,
an oval mirror, snapshots, horn vases (indigo),
dolls, a lamp, a kettle, a north-facing window
that opens up onto a tired, wintry garden
the whites, the blacks, the oaks, the axe.

The poet's room is like any other room
except that when the poet no longer has
a need for it (yes, in *that* way) and it's handed on
to someone else, the poet's still there, for
the words don't cease and the need for them
is as great as ever and the unborn
have a right to a true accounting.

St. Petersburg to Vancouver
December 27, 2013

NOTES

"It is you again, overcoming beauty . . ." The opening lines of Sorley
MacLean's "A Girl and Old Songs." MacLean, *White-Leaping
Flame: Collected Poems*, 224–25.

For Tom
The text for a song written in collaboration with composer Stefan
Smulovitz to honour the life and passionate curiosity of our
friend Tom Cone.

"my pavilion is draped with lungs"
"the Doug Cranmer exhibition." This tribute to Kwakwa̲ka̲'wakw
artist Doug Cranmer, entitled *Kesu': The Art and Life of Doug
Cranmer*, was organized by the UBC Museum of Anthropol-
ogy and exhibited from March 16 to September 3, 2012. I was
powerfully moved, when I first entered the gallery, to hear
Charlie Parker in the air. Cranmer used to listen to Parker
while he worked.

"lightning-gleams / hidden deep within." This phrase is taken
from Kalidasa's ravishing poem *"Meghadutam"* or "The Cloud
Messenger." The poem's narrator sends a cloud endowed
with divinity to reassure his beloved, who is far away, of
his unabated desire for her. Kalidasa may have lived during
the first or second century BCE in Ujjain, Madhya Pradesh.
Kalidasa, 160.

there are lost languages
*"An Italian Fascist told the Rev. H. W. Fox of a serious weakness in
Italian life . . ."* This account was originally published in the
London Spectator on February 6, 1932, and was reproduced in
Gaetano Salvemini's anti-Fascist text *Under the Axe of Fascism*,
published in 1936. The quotation refers to the *"Dopolavoro,"*
the national welfare organization introduced by Mussolini's
government to provide recreational activities for Italian work-
ers during their non-working hours, thereby restricting their
time for political activity. Salvemini, 366–67.

imperium
A prototype: the creeping buttercup, *Ranunculus repens*.

A shore, or Colin in Dogtown
Harold Ross was the founder and editor-in-chief of the *New Yorker*
from 1925 until his death in 1951. The anecdotes are drawn from
James Thurber's indispensable memoir, *The Years with Ross*.

"The Poet" is Charles Olson, who moved to Gloucester, Massa-
chusetts, in 1957.

Sorley MacLean, or Somhairle MacGill-Eain. The most admired and accomplished Gaelic poet of his generation. The excerpts are drawn from his poem "Hallaig," first published in 1954. From the time he was twenty-one, MacLean composed only in Gaelic, later translating his poems into English. In the introduction to his 1991 collection, *From Wood to Ridge: Collected Poems in Gaelic and English*, he writes: "Up to the Second World War, there were in Raasay many of the native birches, hazels, rowans, elders and planted conifers of many kinds, and also a relatively large area of deciduous trees, beeches, chestnuts, elms, ash, oaks, thujas, aspens – even eucalyptus, planted by a wealthy English family of landlords from 1875 onwards. With the War they were nearly all cut down, and replaced by quick-growing conifers. I soon became very fond of the 'old woods' of Raasay . . ." In the poem "Hallaig," he observes, "the symbolism was double or even triple." MacLean, *From Wood to Ridge*, xv.

The Marshalls, Laurence and Lorna, and their children Elizabeth and John, travelled to the Kalahari in the 1950s and early 1960s to study and live among the Ju/'hoansi !Kung, or Bushmen, in Southwest Africa. Over the years they shot thousands of photographs and thousands of feet of film as well as writing and publishing books based on their experiences and field notes. I encountered /Qui's puzzled reaction to the Polaroid multiple of himself at the 2011 exhibition, *From Daguerreotype to Digital: Anthropology and Photography*, at the Peabody Museum of Archaeology and Ethnology at Harvard University.

D. H. Lawrence's description of "the Indian races" appeared posthumously in an article entitled "New Mexico" in *Survey Graphic* in May 1931. Lawrence, 146.

André Breton. Poet, pamphleteer, critic, artist, collector of Indigenous art, author in 1924 of the first Surrealist Manifesto and the conscience of Surrealism thereafter. *Arcane 17*, composed in the Gaspésie in 1944 during a three-month sojourn with his wife-to-be, Elisa Claro, was first published in New York on December 30, 1944, in a limited edition by Brentano's, Inc., and included four full-colour tarot cards designed by Roberto Matta Echaurren. The trade edition, published in April 1945, was to be exhibited in the window of Brentano's bookstore on Fifth Avenue. Marcel Duchamp and Breton got together to create a provocative window display with assistance from the artist and collector Enrico Donati, who devised a memorable sculpture entitled *Feet after Magritte*. With its decapitated mannequin and a poster by Matta of a couple making love, the window display outraged passersby and the bookstore ordered it dismantled before it was completed. It was moved around the corner to the Gotham Book Mart on West 47th Street, where Duchamp called it *Lazy Hardware*. The photo with the reflections of Breton and Duchamp in the window at the Gotham Book Mart was taken by filmmaker Maya Deren.

Breton's *Le surréalisme et la peinture* was originally published in Paris in 1928 and republished in an expanded edition by Brentano's in 1945, the cover of which reproduced Magritte's well-known painting of boots growing toes – or is it toes growing boots?

Leon Battista Alberti's *De pictura* (1435) has been called "the most important theoretical work on the visual arts of the early Renaissance." It was translated into Italian by the author in 1436. Ackerman, 9–11.

"Freud to Jung . . . 1909." According to Jacques Lacan, this anecdote was reported to him when he visited Carl Jung at Küssnacht, near Zurich, in 1954, and it has since been widely circulated. Lacan saw an example of Freud's hubris in these words "whose antiphrasis and gloom do not extinguish their troubled brightness." "The Freudian Thing, or the Meaning of the Return to Freud in Psychoanalysis" in Lacan, 116.

Lexicographer, writer, critic, and talker Samuel Johnson travelled through the western islands of Scotland with his Scottish biographer James Boswell in the fall of 1773. Johnson, 57–58, 97.

"Hopi Indian rabbits' feet." The aerial clutchers of the rabbit's feet on November 7, 1934, were the American writer Gertrude Stein and her companion, Alice B. Toklas. They were off to attend a performance of *Four Saints in Three Acts* – libretto by Stein, music by Virgil Thomson – in Chicago. Wagner-Martin, 213, and Rogers, 130.

the fire

The Blything Union Workhouse at Bulcamp near Blythburgh in Suffolk, England, was funded by 46 nearby parishes and opened in 1766 to house those who for various reasons were not able to support themselves or their families. It was the site of the Bulcamp Riots before it was even built, and unrest continued throughout its existence as a workhouse and as a precursor to Canadian residential and industrial schools. In 1766 it admitted 56 "paupers." By the following year there were 352 "inmates." Clare, 56–57.

"*les Chaudières*." As the story goes, *les Chaudières* – soldiers of the Régiment de la Chaudière – stormed the chateau in Boulogne-sur-Mer in northern France by means of a hidden tunnel. They

succeeded in surprising and imprisoning the Nazis who had
made the castle their headquarters. The city was secured for
the Allies on September 22, 1944, and apparently no one has
discovered the tunnel since. The regimental commandant of *les
Chaudières* during the war was my relative, Lieutenant-Colonel
Paul Mathieu. The chateau's museum contains a fine collection
of Greek, Etruscan, and Egyptian objects and the largest,
most significant group of Aluutiq/Sugpiak masks in existence,
which were hidden away during the war.

"a word is not a vessel"

In Asheville, North Carolina, on the edge of Cherokee territory, a
touring exhibition of Buddhist relics was displayed in a former
workshop in the centre of town at the beginning of November
2014. Many of the relics are those of revered saints. The boy is
a magical boy associated with the origins of Cherokee culture.

The "Haida painter" is the artist Charles Edenshaw, who spent
over a week with anthropologist Franz Boas in Port Essington,
British Columbia, in August 1897 during the first summer of
the Jesup North Pacific Expedition, making drawings and
paintings and identifying masks and regalia in the American
Museum of Natural History and in other museums. It was
during this encounter that Edenshaw, speaking in Chinook
jargon, told Boas the origin story in which the Raven releases
the boisterous first people from a cockleshell. Boas, 223–28,
and Swanton, 320.

"We are like goats tied to the butcher's stake . . ." Hochschild, 257.

Root Map

Many thanks to Makiko Hara, Carmen Lam, Paul Plimley, and
Annabel Vaughan and to Centre A for commissioning this
work. It has been altered from its first performance.

"Embassy Café." A "Chinese-Canadian" restaurant on Fisgard
Street in Victoria's Chinatown, no longer in operation.

"Whisky per tutti!" From the libretto by Guelfo Civinini and
Carlo Zangarini for Puccini's opera *La Fanciulla del West*
(1910). When asked confidentially by several miners at *La
Polka* if their beloved Minnie has asked for them by name,
the bartender nods, puts on a conspiratorial air, and says
yes, indeed she has. The lovesick miners respond by buying
a round of drinks or cigars for the house. *La Fanciulla del
West* was based on David Belasco's play *The Girl of the Golden
West* (1905). Belasco arrived in British Columbia as a boy and
lived with his family in Victoria and in Barkerville during
the gold rush.

"Boy Cornwell." Jack Cornwell was a boy seaman aboard the HMS
   Chester during the Battle of Jutland. As boys ourselves, we
   admired him fiercely for his courage and sense of duty. During
   the battle he was assigned to one of the gun emplacements,
   and after the entire gun crew had been wiped out due to shrap-
   nel – the result of criminally thoughtless design – he manned
   the position until he was mortally wounded himself. He died
   on June 2, 1916, and was posthumously awarded a Victoria
   Cross for his courage and his refusal to leave his position.

"Bonhomme, les canots." The references are to the *Carnaval d'hiver*
   each February in Quebec City and the boat races across the
   ice floes and open water of the St. Lawrence.

"Universal Change." Before human beings became earth-, water-,
   and sky-shaping creatures, they were preceded by animals
   who were human in form and who could speak to one another.
   Although they were not all bad, the animals proved to be
   as greedy and sneaky and envious and violent as humans
   have become, with the result that they had to relinquish
   their grip on the world. The Universal Change refers to the
   moment when humans succeeded them. I often reflect on
   the night before they all scuttled into the sea or the bush
   to become the creatures we know now, before they lost
   their language. It must have been a night of reckoning, of
   tears, of acknowledgement, of reminiscing, and of moving,
   rueful farewells.

rideau

"Tropic of Cancer." A novel by American writer Henry Miller, first
   published in Paris in 1934. Rather than allowing us to read
   the copy she'd secretly acquired, my friend Willy's older sister
   ran down to the Rideau Canal in Ottawa and threw the "por-
   nographic" book into the water. I watched helplessly from a
   bridge as the current carried it toward Dow's Lake.

"hawk-eyed Monty." When I was an army cadet in Ottawa,
   Field-Marshall Bernard Montgomery, known to us as Monty,
   the hero of Alamein, visited the school and inspected our
   cadet corps, looking at a new young hatch of souls to thresh.

"Peggy Lee Band." A small ensemble made up of some of the best
   improvising jazz musicians in Vancouver and led by the bril-
   liant composer and cello player Peggy Lee. "Floating Island"
   is a track on the CD entitled *New Code* issued in 2008, with
   Jeremy Berkman, trombone; André Lachance, bass; Peggy
   Lee, cello; Ron Samworth, guitar; Brad Turner, flugelhorn,
   trumpet; Dylan van der Schyff, drums.

Elementary Mensuration

"*The object of the present work . . .*" Septimus Tebay, Preface to
*Elementary Mensuration for the Use of Schools with Numerous
Examples*, v–vi.

"or a vine blooming with birds' / beaks and sober, snouted crea-
tures." A reference to the *waqwaq*: "Supposedly, during the
course of his apocryphal Eastern adventures, Alexander came
upon the oracular talking tree, the *waqwaq*, from the foliage
of which sprouted masks similar to those seen in [the Divan
of Sultan Husayn Bayqara], warning him against trying to
conquer India." Welch, 92–93.

a conversation

The story in question, entitled "Adventure of a Couple in Love,"
can be found in Himmelheber, 98. It reads, in its entirety:
"He went with her on a walk in the tundra. It was evening.
Suddenly a huge wolf was standing in front of them with its
jaws greedily gaping wide. The woman had the marvellous idea
to tear her clothes from her body, and thus she stood totally
naked in front of the monster. Rooted on the spot by surprise,
the wolf could not move. Curious things had occurred in
his life already, but he had never seen such a strange thing!"

"forget the rubber paddles"

"a crazed pinch-hitter scrawls on a tree parasite." This figure,
first drawn on a bracket fungus by the Raven, and known
today as Fungus, or the Fungus Man, is brought to life in
an act of desperation, or so we're told in the Haida epic
Raven Travelling. The Raven has been trying for some time to
provide his wife and his sister with the parts they're missing,
which are found on a dangerous, rocky shoal. He has enlisted
the help of many birds and other creatures, but as they near
the shoal, the animals fall haplessly into an erotic swoon
and prove incapable of keeping the unsteady canoe on its
course. The Fungus, wedged into the stern of the canoe,
proves to be a single-minded and accomplished helmsman,
and the Raven's quest is successful, thereby assuring the
future of the race. gid7ahl-gudsllay, lalaxaaygans, Terri-Lynn
Williams-Davidson, "How Raven Gave Females Their Tsaw,"
in Wright and Augaitis with Davidson and Hart, 61. Also
Swanton, 126, and Bringhurst, 281, 483. The journey of the
Raven and the Fungus is brilliantly commemorated on three
platters carved by Charles Edenshaw during the 1880s.

swan

Inspired by "The Crucifixion," a twelfth-century English song,
"swan" was set to music by Alex Mah and performed at the
Djavad Mowafaghian World Art Centre at the SFU School

for the Contemporary Arts on April 11, 2013, as part of "Art Song 2013 – SFU Composers in Concert." The musicians were Heather Pawsey, soprano; Melanie Adams, mezzo-soprano; Marcus Takizawa, viola; and Tina Chang, piano. Many thanks to Alex Mah and Professor David MacIntyre.

granny soot

Granny Soot is a witch in the novel *Mulata de tal*, or, in its English translation, *Mulata*, by Guatemalan novelist Miguel Ángel Asturias, first published in 1963. It was also the name of a cottage on the West Saanich Road near Mount Newton on Vancouver Island.

"a British drunk" refers to Malcolm Lowry, author of *Under the Volcano* (1947), written while Lowry lived at Dollarton, just outside Vancouver, on the shore of Burrard Inlet.

"*Keaton once told me that he and Chaplin missed the sound of the camera cranking . . .*" Gilliatt, 147.

a surgeon

The surgeon is the Montreal physician, surgeon, and inventor of the mobile blood-transfusion unit, Norman Bethune, who, at the conclusion of a cross-Canada tour in 1937, to the delight of his enemies, declared publicly that he was a Communist. Arriving in Victoria from Vancouver on the midnight Canadian Pacific Railway (CPR) boat, he asked to be taken to Thetis Lake, where he spent the day alone on an isolated island. When he returned to shore late in the afternoon, he'd made up his mind to leave Canada and to join Mao Zedong's Long March in China. That night, surprisingly, given his Communist credentials, Bethune addressed the Victoria Chamber of Commerce. Peck, 64–67.

The Consul is Geoffrey Firmin, the central character in Malcolm Lowry's novel *Under the Volcano*. As the novel opens, Jacques Laruelle, a filmmaker and an acquaintance of the Consul, is reflecting on the final lines of Christopher Marlowe's *Doctor Faustus*, a play he'd borrowed from the Consul the year before. The lines lead Laruelle to contemplate, once again, the Consul's violent, useless death.

"*Terminat hora diem; / terminat auctor opus.*" These lines conclude *Doctor Faustus*, and can be translated as "The hour completes the day; the author concludes his work." *Doctor Faustus* was possibly first performed in London in 1592, and was published in 1604. Christopher Marlowe, its author, was stabbed to death under still mysterious circumstances.

"*viri a diis recentes . . .*" These words can be translated as "men fresh from the gods" or "men freshly minted by the gods."

In his essay "On the Cannibals," Michel de Montaigne is, in this observation, quoting Seneca, *Epist. Moral., XC*, 44. The first edition of de Montaigne's *Essais* was published in 1580 and he continued to revise the book until the end of his life. This phrase, describing the inhabitants of America, had been added to the text he was working on not long before he died. de Montaigne, 84.

the hatch

Paul Éluard. Pseudonym of Eugène Grindel. French poet, critic, and collector, associated with André Breton and others connected to Surrealism during the 1920s and early 1930s. In the late 1930s, Éluard joined the Communist Party, which led to a permanent split between himself and Breton. Perhaps Éluard's best-known poem, published in 1942, is "*Liberté.*"

"*We have not learned to be wary of the beatific smile of fraternity.*" This warning is from Alain Finkielkraut's 1989 *Remembering in Vain: The Klaus Barbie Trial and Crimes against Humanity.* Barbie was tried for war crimes, in Lyons, France, during the summer of 1987. Finkielkraut, 58.

"the morning he brought her down in Brentwood Bay." On March 3, 1919, Eddie Hubbard became the first aviator to fly the mail from Seattle to Victoria and back again. He made regular trips thereafter, and one morning landed in the middle of Brentwood Bay in the Saanich Inlet north of Victoria. My grandparents were living in Brentwood Bay at the time and witnessed the miraculous descent of an aircraft that stayed afloat. Fearing that they might never see such a contraption again, my grandmother, Nora, tossed her three little girls into a boat and rowed out to touch the mysterious seaplane. "You can tell your grandchildren," she said.

"*It has always been a protest, however ineffectual, against myth, against a fate which was always the same.*" An influential theorist of dialectics and writer on music, Theodor Adorno was the director of the Institute for Social Research at the University of Frankfurt from 1956–1969. Adorno, 151.

Wilson Duff. Canadian anthropologist, archaeologist, and curator in Victoria and Vancouver who had a special feeling for the masterful sculpture of Haida artist da.a.xiigang Charles Edenshaw.

"*I do not want to be forced to put on the glove of a skeleton . . .*" This refusal is from Antonin Artaud's incendiary letter to André Breton, written in February 1947 in response to Breton's invitation to participate in the 1947 International Surrealist Exhibition. Artaud, n.p.

"the drones, Helen tells me"
Three common elements found in meteorites: Fe (iron), Co (cobalt), and Ni (nickel).

"in the oak grove"
In 1913, the British Board of Film Censors seized a film which, it declared, had been "calculated to demoralize the public." The offending scenes were cut. The BBFC, which had been established the year before, was an industry association and had no statutory power. It seemed to recognize from the beginning that its members would be less harassed by indignant moralists if they served up their own scapegoats from time to time.

"Intoxicated by the heady wine of newly acquired power . . ."
Swami Vivekananda quoted in *London Review of Books* 33, no. 21 (November 3, 2011): 11. Review of Niall Ferguson's *Civilisation: The West and the Rest* (London: Allen Lane, 2011).

"Cendrars, in 1912"
Blaise Cendrars, French poet and novelist. Cendrars, *Le Transsibérien*. For an account of his experiences at the front during the First World War, see "Shadows in the Darkness" in Cendrars, *Sky*, 191–207.

"I am talking about . . ." Césaire, *Discourse on Colonialism*, 43. Born in Martinique, Aimé Césaire was a poet, editor, activist, and politician, becoming the Communist mayor of Fort-de-France and a deputy in the French Assembly before rejecting Stalinism in 1956. He devised the term "Negritude" and worked tirelessly to expose the violence and brutality of colonialism in all its disguises.

Haiti
"poète et *prince."* The *poète* is André Breton who with his new wife, Elisa, arrived in Haiti, en route to Europe, in December 1945 and stayed for a little over a month. His interviews and lecture on Surrealism contributed to the unrest already present among Haitian students and workers who, in the days to follow, organized strikes and riots that led to the flight of the dictator and his replacement by a revolutionary government.

"the Rex." Breton delivered his lecture "Le Surréalisme" or "Surrealism and Haiti" at the Rex Cinema in Port-au-Prince on December 20, 1945. Paul Laraque, "André Breton in Haiti" in Richardson, 217–28.

"Malcolm." Malcolm Lowry stopped off in Haiti with his wife, Marjorie, almost a year after Breton, on their way to New York for the launch of *Under the Volcano* in 1947. Sigbjørn Wilderness is the central character in Malcolm Lowry's short story "Strange Comfort Afforded by the Profession" (1953). He also appears in the short stories "Through the Panama" and "Gin and Goldenrod," and he was to be at the heart of Lowry's planned six-novel suite, *The Voyage That Never Ends*. Freighters churn throughout these stories, their engines singing what Wilderness in "Through the Panama" calls "the ship's endless song." Sigurd, the narrator of "The Bravest Boat," is reminded of the thrum of a freighter's engines – "*Frère* Jacques! *Frère* Jacques!" – and asks, "What strange poem of God's mercy was this?" Lowry, *Hear Us O Lord from Heaven Thy Dwelling Place* and *Lunar Caustic*, 21.

"*he almost manages / to bring beauty / back to life again.*" In a long dialogue that concludes *Introduction to Modernity* (1962), Henri Lefebvre's "Mr. B." likens Malcolm Lowry's achievement to that of Picasso, praising his novel *Under the Volcano*. "Twelfth Prelude: Towards a New Romanticism?" in Lefebvre, 352.

"a square of light"
Dedicated to the memory of Tom Cone.

"Cendrars's right hand." On September 28, 1915, Blaise Cendrars, who had joined the French Foreign Legion, was severely injured in the battle for Navarin Farm in Champagne, France. As a result he lost his right arm and had to learn to write with his left hand, which he called "*la main amie.*" Cendrars, *Complete Poems*, xvii.

"Jeffers's '*cloud of men's palms*'." The phrase is taken from "Hands" by the American poet Robinson Jeffers. Jeffers, 128.

"Montmartre." The reference is to a question repeatedly asked by la Petite Jeanne in *Prose du Transsibérien et de la Petite Jeanne de France*: "*Blaise, dis, somme-nous bien loin de Montmartre?*" Cendrars, *Du Monde Entier au Coeur du Monde: Poèmes de Blaise Cendrars*, 43.

"our *grande ourse* – / Desnos's bear." The reference is to the poem "*L'ours*" ("The Bear") by French poet Robert Desnos. Desnos, 1339.

"*star people.*" I learned the expression "star people" from a woman making and selling jewellery in a parking-lot market in Merritt, British Columbia, in the fall of 2013.

"twenty-two thousand seabirds"
"*Everything smells of feathers.*" Fernandez-Arnesto, 279.

form
The subject is Orpheus, who came to a bad end when he turned his back on the gods and the women who desired him.

"Then I took a mistress, and she bore me a son, who grew up to look like a slice of the moon." *The Arabian Nights, Based on the text of the Fourteenth-Century Syrian Manuscript edited by Muhsin Mahdi,* 22.

"Buffy Sainte-Marie"
Singer-songwriter and activist, born on the Piapot Cree reserve in Saskatchewan.

"Sandy at the kitchen"
The fine Scottish poet, singer, and translator, Alexander Hutchison, born in Buckie, Scotland.

"what we call / the Modern"
Franz Boas, anthropologist; Sigmund Freud, psychoanalyst; Claude Lévi-Strauss, anthropologist; André Breton, poet and critic. These are my scavengers of paradise whose terrestrial, psychic, and metaphorical archaeologies laid the foundation for the Modern.

Klee Wyck
"First we must study how colonization works to decivilize *the colonizer . . ."* Césaire, *Discourse on Colonialism,* 35.

"Your silent Indian will teach you more than all the art jargon . . ." Carr, *Growing Pains: The Autobiography of Emily Carr,* 220.

Emily Carr's *"NO."* See "Friends" in Carr, *Klee Wyck,* 114. Her friend Ira Dilworth, in the foreword to the 1941 edition: "*Klee Wyck* is made up of sketches written at various times and brought together and published now for the first time. Long ago, when it was her habit to go into wild, lonely places seeking Indian subjects, Miss Carr's artist mind received impressions which have remained sharp and real for her across the years. By fish-boat, gas-boat, sometimes by Indian canoe, taking with her a few books, at least one dog and her sketching kit, she penetrated forest and village on the British Columbia coast, even going on occasion over to the Queen Charlottes. The vivid images stored then in her mind have been brooded over since by her rich imaginative faculty and the result is an unusual collection of sketches in words, not paint." Carr, *Klee Wyck,* 18–19.

"to a nation . . . and its poets." One of the nation's poets, Duncan Campbell Scott, was superintendent of education and deputy superintendent general of the Department of Indian Affairs from 1909 to 1931. Carr's concern in "Friends" about tuberculosis was well founded. In 1909 Scott admitted as much to his superior: "If the schools are to be conducted at all we must face the fact that a large number of the pupils will suffer from tuberculosis in some of its various forms. The admission indiscriminately of such pupils into the schools in the past, and the failure to recognize any special treatment which could be accorded to them has no doubt led to the high death rate which has rendered ineffectual to a large degree the past expenditure on Indian education in Boarding and Industrial schools. More stringent regulations as to the admission of pupils will doubtless have a beneficial effect, and it is only necessary to carry out some common sense reforms to remove the imputation that the Department is careless of the interests of these children." Scott's apparent concern for the reputation for the schools over the welfare of the children provides a distressing insight into the administration of the residential and industrial schools in the year that Marinetti first published the *Futurist Manifesto*. Titley, 85.

"to the editor who after Carr's death censored 2,300 words . . ." The editor of Clarke, Irwin, the Toronto publisher of the "Canadian Classics" edition of *Klee Wyck* in 1951, was William Clarke. It was his intention to publish an "educational edition" for Canadian schools, which, at the time, were often affiliated with religious institutions. The omitted passages usually express Carr's dismay at the behaviour of missionaries and other religious zealots. In the chapter entitled "Martha's Joey," which was cut entirely, a priest has paid a visit to a Native woman named Martha, seized her child, and "sent him way to school." With her mother, young Emily visits Martha and finds her weeping and dishevelled. Emily's mother tells her: "It's beastly of the priest to steal him from Martha." The account concludes with a single sentence: "Martha cried till she had no more tears and then she died." Carr, *Klee Wyck*, 116–17.

"I think you should certainly proceed with the experimental work on gas bombs . . ." Churchill quoted in Baker, 7.

sanctuaries

"Trees hold us all together." Toward the end of her life, my mother, Kythé, would sometimes wake up out of a deep sleep and make a statement that was almost always profound and often apropos. One afternoon in November 2004 she surprised us with this observation.

"lake of blood." Leonardo de Vinci: "If a man has a lake of blood in him whereby the lungs expand and contract in breathing, the earth's body has its oceanic sea which likewise expands and contracts every six hours as the earth breathes" (Ms. A, fol. 564v). Ackerman, 158.

"recalling / the poet's hand . . ." The poet is Blaise Cendrars.

pemberton valley

Three young CBC Vancouver filmmakers travelled to the small
town of Pemberton early in 1957 to explore the possibility of
an hour-long broadcast documentary film. The finished film
begins as a hymn to spring and the joys of children released
from winter in the Pemberton Valley depicted through the
lives of a Lil'wat family at Mount Currie and a non-Native
family residing nearby. *The Pemberton Valley* was broadcast by
CBUT on April 10, 1958. Many thanks to George Roberston for
elements of this account and to Colin Preston, irreplaceable
CBC Vancouver librarian and archivist, for providing me with
a copy of this complex film.

"For a man taking stock of himself . . ." Breton, *Arcane 17*, 36: *"pour
l'homme pris isolément il ne saurait y avoir d'espoir plus valable
et plus étendu que dans le coup d'aile."* For an English language
edition, see Breton, *Arcanum 17*, 55. I have adapted the trans-
lation from that text.

four men

"la Section d'Or." Opened in Paris on October 9, 1912, *Le salon de la
section d'or* was, in the words of Calvin Tomkins, "the largest
and most important of the pre-war Cubist group exhibitions,"
although it was ignored by Picasso and Braque. Six paintings
by Duchamp were exhibited, including *Nude Descending a
Staircase, No. 2*; *Portrait of Chess Players*; *The King and Queen
Surrounded by Swift Nudes*; and *The King and Queen Traversed
by Nudes at High Speed*. Tomkins, 103–104.

Francis Picabia. A prolific artist of French-Cuban descent, editor
of the journal *391*, and a participant in the Dada and Surrealist
movements in Paris. Gabrielle Buffet, Picabia's wife, was a
composer, a writer, a critic, and a chronicler of the avant-garde.

"une machine / à 5 coeurs." Duchamp, *Notes*, 68. The five passengers
left Paris on the stormy night of October 20, 1912.

"a bracket fungus." This alludes to the Raven's helmsman, Fungus,
or Fungus Man, who, wedged into the stern of the canoe,
helped Raven successfully approach the dangerous shoal
to capture the life-bringing part. Wright and Augaitis with
Davidson and Hart, 61. Also Swanton, 126, and Bringhurst,
281, 483.

"A la fin tu es las / de ce monde ancien." These are the opening
lines of Guillaume Apollinaire's celebrated 1912 poem "Zone."
Apollinaire, 2.

"l'enfant-Dieu, // rappelant assez le Jésus / des primitifs . . ."
Duchamp, *Notes*, 68.

"the child, he muses, / "could ... be a comet ..." Duchamp, *Salt Seller: The Writings of Marcel Duchamp (Marchand du Sel)*, 26.

"Painting is finished." Ades, Cox, and Hopkins, 69. Tomkins, 113.

the lane

"*In the vast colony of our being ...*" Pessoa, 328, text 396: "Each of us is several, is many, is a profusion of selves. So that the self who disdains his surroundings is not the same as the self who suffers or takes joy in them. In the vast colony of our being there are many species of people who think and feel in different ways."

"Nootka rose." *Rosa nutkana*, often called a wild rose, is a tall, sweetly and pungently scented perennial shrub in the rose family (*Rosaceae*). Its petals are both light and dark pink with a yellow centre. It often grows along shorelines, and its height is determined by the nature of its location. Europeans first encountered the species at what they called Nootka Sound on Vancouver Island's west coast in the eighteenth century.

Pellegrino Turri built the first working typewriter in 1808 so that his blind lover, Countess Carolina Fantoni da Fivizzano, could write him letters. Ink was supplied by means of carbon paper, which he invented for the purpose.

The *Sv. Nikolai* sailed from New Arkhangel, today's Sitka, Alaska, on September 29, 1808. An account of the voyage can be found in Owens, *The Wreck of the Sv. Nikolai*.

The Last Judgement (1808) is the great vision of the end of the world painted by William Blake, British poet, artist, and visionary.

"*5 patterned blankets ...*" Owens, 64.

American composer Philip Glass, speaking with CBC Radio's Eleanor Wachtel before the world premiere of his *String Quartet No. 6* by the Kronos Quartet at the Chan Centre for the Performing Arts, Vancouver, on October 19, 2013.

"I do not fear death." Owens, 60.

John McKay, MacKay, MacCay, McKey, M'Key, or MacKoy. Bumstead, n.p.; Gunther, 91, 193; Hoover, 69–106; and Owens, 24.

"Yuquot." A Mowachaht/Muchalaht village on the west coast of Vancouver Island at the mouth of what is now called Nootka Sound. James Cook named the village Friendly Cove when he visited in 1778.

"fulmar / beaks." Korsun, Berezkin, and Kupina, xxix.

Dachau was constructed in 1933 as a suburb of Munich. It was the first major concentration camp established by the Nazis and became the model for the camps that followed. In July 1945, Benjamin Britten and Yehudi Menuhin were invited to travel to the extermination camps in Europe to play duets for the inmates. Mehuhin played the violin; Britten played the piano. They performed at Bergen-Belsen soon after it was liberated and the experience was shattering. Britten was unable to speak about it when he returned to England. No itinerary of the tour remains according to the Britten-Pears Foundation archive in Aldeburgh, Suffolk, although it's understood that the two men visited several camps during the weeks they were away.

"*Qu'y puis-je?*" Césaire, "En guise de manifeste littéraire" (1942) in *Cahier d'un retour au pays natal*, 71. The text was first published in Paris in the journal *Volontés* in August 1939. Césaire, *Return to My Native Land*, 60. The translation below is by Anna Bostock and John Berger:

What can I do?
I must begin.
Begin what?
The only thing in the world that's worth beginning:
The End of the World, *no less!*

The poet's room (Anna Akhmatova)
The quotation is from Part Three, the "Epilogue" to Anna Akhmatova's "A Poem Without a Hero: A Tryptich," translated by Carl R. Proffer with Assya Humesky. The maple tree is one of many in the garden of the Sheremetev Palace, known to Akhmatova's readers as the House on the Fontanka. Proffer, 222.

SOURCES

Ackerman, James S. *Origins, Imitation, Conventions: Representation in the Visual Arts.* Cambridge, MA: The MIT Press, 2002.

Ades, Dawn, Neil Cox, and David Hopkins. *Marcel Duchamp.* London: Thames & Hudson, 1999.

Adorno, Theodor. *Quasi Una Fantasia: Essays on Modern Music.* London: Verso: 2011.

Akhmatova, Anna. "A Poem Without a Hero." Trans. Carl R. Proffer with Assya Humesky. Carl R. Proffer and Ellendea Proffer, eds. *The Silver Age of Russian Culture.* Ann Arbor: Ardis, 1975.

Apollinaire, Guillaume. *Alcools.* Trans. Anne Hyde Greet. Foreword Warren Ramsey. Berkeley: University of California Press, 1965.

The Arabian Nights, Based on the text of the Fourteenth-Century Syrian Manuscript edited by Muhsin Mahdi. Trans. Husain Haddawy. New York: W. W. Norton, 1990.

Artaud, Antonin. "Letter to André Breton." Trans. Clayton Eshleman. Los Angeles: Black Sparrow Press, Sparrow 23, 1974.

Baker, Nicholson. *Human Smoke: The Beginnings of World War II, the End of Civilization.* New York: Simon & Schuster, 2008.

Benjamin, Walter. "On Some Motifs in Baudelaire." In *Selected Writings, Volume 4, 1938–1940.* Ed. Howard Eiland and Michael W. Jennings. Trans. Edmund Jephcott *et al.* Cambridge, MA: The Belknap Press of Harvard University Press, 2003.

Blanchot, Maurice. *The Instant of My Death.* / Derrida, Jacques. *Demeure: Fiction and Testimony.* Trans. Elizabeth Rottenberg. Stanford: Stanford University Press, 2000.

Blom, Philipp. *The Vertigo Years: Change and Culture in the West, 1900–1914.* Toronto: Emblem / McClelland & Stewart, 2008.

Boas, Franz. *The Ethnography of Franz Boas: Letters and Diaries of Franz Boas Written on the Northwest Coast from 1886 to 1931.* Comp. and ed. Ronald P. Rohner. Intro. Ronald P. Rohner and Evelyn C. Rohner. Trans. Hedy Parker. Chicago: University of Chicago Press, 1969.

Breton, André. "Speech to Young Haitian Poets." In *What Is Surrealism? Selected Writings.* Ed. and intro. Franklin Rosemont. New York: Pathfinder, 2008.

——. *Arcanum 17.* Trans. Zack Rogow. Intro. Anna Balakian. Copenhagen: Green Integer, 2004.

——. *Surrealism and Painting.* Trans. Simon Watson Taylor. Intro. Mark Polizzotti. Boston: MFA Publications, 2002.

——. *Arcane 17.* Paris: Jean-Jacques Pauvert éditeur, 1971.

——. *Le surréalisme et la peinture.* 2nd ed. New York: Brentano's, 1945.

Bringhurst, Robert. *A Story as Sharp as a Knife: The Classical Haida Mythtellers and Their World.* 2nd ed. Vancouver: Douglas & McIntyre, 2011.

Bumstead, J. M. "MacKay, John," in *Dictionary of Canadian Biography Online*, vol. 4, University of Toronto / Université Laval, Biographi.ca, 2003–.

Carr, Emily. *Klee Wyck.* Forewords Ira Dilworth. Intro. Kathryn Bridge. Vancouver: Douglas & McIntyre, 2003.

——. *Growing Pains: The Autobiography of Emily Carr.* 2nd ed. Toronto: Clarke, Irwin, 1966.

Cendrars, Blaise. *Complete Poems.* Intro. Jay Bochner. Trans. Ron Padgett. Berkeley: University of California Press, 1992.

——. *Sky: Memoirs.* Trans. Nina Rootes. Intro. Marjorie Perloff. New York: Paragon House, 1992.

——. *Du monde entier au coeur du monde: Poèmes de Blaise Cendrars.* Paris: Editions Denoël, 1957.

——. *Le Transsibérien.* Paris: Pierre Seghers, 1966.

Césaire, Aimé. *Discourse on Colonialism* (1950). Trans. Joan Pinkham. New York: Monthly Review Press, 2000.

——. *Cahier d'un retour au pays natal.* Paris: Présence Africaine, 1983.

——. *Return to My Native Land.* Intro. Mazisi Kunene. Trans. Anna Bostock and John Berger. Harmondsworth: Penguin, 1969.

Chevigny, Hector. *Russian America: The Great Alaskan Venture, 1741–1867.* Portland, OR: Binford & Mort, 1979.

Clare, Rev. J. B. *Wenhaston and Bulcamp, Suffolk, Curious Parish Records and Workhouse Riots with Description of the Recently Discovered Ancient Painting of "The Wenhaston Doom."* Halesworth: William P. Gale, 1903.

Conley, Katharine. *Robert Desnos, Surrealism, and the Marvellous in Everyday Life.* Lincoln: University of Nebraska Press, 2003.

de Montaigne, Michel. "On the Cannibals." Trans. and ed. M. A. Screech. *The Essays: A Selection.* London: Penguin, 2004.

Desnos, Robert. *Robert Desnos: Oeuvres,* établie et présentée par Marie-Claire Dumas. Paris: Quarto Gallimard, 2011.

Duchamp, Marcel. *Notes.* Avant-propos Paul Matisse. Préface Pontius Hulten. Paris: Flammarion / Champs arts, 1999.

——. *Salt Seller: The Writings of Marcel Duchamp (Marchand du sel).* Ed. Michel Sanouillet and Elmer Peterson. New York: Oxford University Press, 1973.

Fernandez-Arnesto, Felipe. *Civilizations: Culture, Ambition, and the Transformation of Nature.* New York: The Free Press, 2001.

Finkielkraut, Alain. *Remembering in Vain: The Klaus Barbie Trial and Crimes against Humanity.* Trans. Roxanne Lapidus with Sima Godfrey. Intro. Alice Y. Kaplan. New York: Columbia University Press, 1992.

Gilliatt, Penelope. *Three-Quarter Face: Reports and Reflections.* New York: Coward, McCann & Geoghegan, 1980.

Gunther, Erna. *Indian Life on the Northwest Coast of North America as Seen by the Early Explorers and Fur Traders during the Last Decades of the Eighteenth Century.* Chicago: University of Chicago Press, 1975.

Himmelheber, Hans. Trans. Kurt and Ester Vitt. Ed. and annot. Ann Fienup-Riordan. *Where the Echo Began and other Oral Traditions from Southwestern Alaska.* Fairbanks: University of Alaska Press, 2000.

Hochschild, Adam. *To End All Wars: A Story of Loyalty and Rebellion, 1914–1918.* New York: Mariner Books / Houghton Mifflin Harcourt, 2012.

Hoover, Alan L., ed. *Nuu-Chah-Nulth Voices: Histories, Objects, and Journeys.* Victoria: Royal British Columbia Museum, 2000.

Igler, David. *The Great Ocean: Pacific Worlds from Captain Cook to the Gold Rush.* Oxford: Oxford University Press, 2013.

Jansen, Bert. "Marcel Duchamp: kunstenaar ~ knutselaar" / "Marcel Duchamp: an artist ~ anartist." Rotterdam: Museum Boijmans Van Beuningen, 2013.

Jeffers, Robinson. *Dear Judas and Other Poems.* Afterword Robert J. Brophy. New York: Liveright, 1977.

Jenness, Diamond. *The Faith of a Coast Salish Indian.* In *Anthropology in British Columbia, Memoirs Nos. 2 and 3.* Ed. Wilson Duff. Victoria: British Columbia Provincial Museum, Department of Education, 1955.

Johnson, Samuel. *A Journey to the Western Islands of Scotland*. Ed. Mary Lascelles. New Haven: Yale University Press, 1971.

Judt, Tony. *Postwar: A History of Europe since 1945*. New York: Penguin, 2005.

Kalidasa. *The Loom of Time: A Selection of His Plays and Poems*. Trans. and intro. Chandra Rajan. New Delhi: Penguin, 1989.

Korsun, S. A., Y. E. Berezkin, and Y. A. Kupina. *The Alutiit/Sugpiat: A Catalogue of the Collections of the Kunstkamera*. Fairbanks: University of Alaska Press, 2012.

Kramer, Jennifer. *Kesu': The Art and Life of Doug Cranmer*. Vancouver: Douglas & McIntyre, 2012.

Lacan, Jacques. *Écrits: A Selection*. Trans. Alan Sheridan. New York: W. W. Norton, 1977.

Laughlin, James, ed. *New Directions in Prose & Poetry 1940*. Norfolk, Connecticut: New Directions, 1940.

Lawrence, D. H. "New Mexico." In *Phoenix: The Posthumous Papers of D. H. Lawrence*. Ed. and intro. Edward D. McDonald. London: William Heinemann, 1936.

Leach, Edmund. *Genesis as Myth and Other Essays*. London: Jonathan Cape, 1969.

Lefebvre, Henri. *Introduction to Modernity: Twelve Preludes, September 1959 – May 1961*. Trans. John Moore. London: Verso, 2011.

Lowry, Malcolm. *Hear Us O Lord From Heaven Thy Dwelling Place* and *Lunar Caustic*. Harmondsworth: Penguin, 1979.

——. *Under the Volcano*. New York: Reynal & Hitchcock, 1947.MacDonald, George F. *Chiefs of the Sea and Sky: Haida Heritage Sites of the Queen Charlotte Islands*. Vancouver: University of British Columbia Press, 1989.

MacLean, Sorley. *White-Leaping Flame: Collected Poems*. Ed. Christopher Whyte and Emma Dymock. Edinburgh: Polygon, 2012.

——. *From Wood to Ridge: Collected Poems in Gaelic and English*. Rev. ed. London: Vintage, 1991.

Marlowe, Christopher. *Doctor Faustus*.

Matthews, Owen. *Glorious Misadventures: Nikolai Rezanov and the Dream of a Russian America*. New York: Bloomsbury, 2013.

Melville, Herman, *The Confidence-Man: His Masquerade*. Ed., intro., and annot. H. Bruce Franklin. Champaign, IL: Dalkey Archive Press, 2007.

Nowell-Smith, Geoffrey, ed. *The Oxford History of World Cinema*. Oxford: Oxford University Press, 1996.

Orledge, Robert. *Satie Remembered*. Trans. Roger Nichols. London: Faber & Faber, 1995.

Owens, Kenneth N., ed. and intro. *The Wreck of the Sv. Nikolai*. Trans. Alton S. Donnelly. Lincoln: University of Nebraska Press, 2001. Includes "The Narrative of Timofei Tarakanov" (1822) and "The Narrative of Ben Hobucket" (1934).

Peck, Mary Biggar. *Red Moon over Spain: Canadian Media Reaction to the Spanish Civil War, 1936–1939*. Ottawa: Steel Rail Publishing, 1988.

Pessoa, Fernando. *The Book of Disquiet*. Ed., trans. and intro. Richard Zenith. London: Penguin, 2001.

Pollizotti, Mark. *Revolution of the Mind: The Life of André Breton*. New York: Farrar, Straus & Giroux, 1995.

Proffer, Carl, and Ellendea Proffer, eds. *The Silver Age of Russian Culture*. Ann Arbor: Ardis, 1975.

Reinhart, Herman Francis. *The Golden Frontier: The Recollections of Herman Francis Reinhart, 1851–1869*. Ed. Doyce B. Nunis Jr. Austin: University of Texas Press, 1962.

Richardson, Michael, ed. *Refusal of the Shadow: Surrealism and the Caribbean.* Trans. Michael Richardson and Krzysztof Fijalkowski. London: Verso, 1996.

Rogers, W. G. *When This You See Remember Me: Gertrude Stein in Person.* New York: Rinehart, 1948.

Rozell, Ned. "Fungus Man and the Start of It All." Fairbanks: University of Alaska Geophysical Institute, Alaska Science Forum, Article 2082, September 20, 2011.

Salvemini, Gaetano. *Under the Axe of Fascism.* London: Victor Gollancz, 1936.

Shostakovich, D. D. *Testimony: The Memoirs of Dmitry Shostakovich as related to and edited by Solomon Volkov.* Ed. Solomon Volkov. Trans. Antonina W. Bouis. New York: Harper & Row, 1979.

Solovyov, Isodor. "The Moon's Sister." Brian Swann, *Coming to Light: Contemporary Translations of the Native Literatures of North America.* New York: Vintage, 1996.

Stafford, Jos. *The Canadian Oyster: Its Development, Environment, and Culture.* Ottawa: Mortimer, 1913.

Studlar, Gaylyn. "Rudolph Valentino." Geoffrey Nowell-Smith, ed. *The Oxford History of World Cinema.* Oxford: Oxford University Press, 1996. 44–45.

Swanton, John Reed. *Haida Texts and Myths, Skidegate Dialect, Recorded by John R. Swanton.* Washington: Smithsonian Institution, *Bureau of American Ethnology Bulletin* 29, 1905.

Tebay, Septimus. *Elementary Mensuration for the Use of Schools with Numerous Examples.* London: Macmillan, 1868.

Thurber, James. *The Years with Ross.* Boston: Little, Brown, 1959.

Titley, E. Brian. *A Narrow Vision: Duncan Campbell Scott and the Administration of Indian Affairs in Canada.* Vancouver: University of British Columbia Press, 1986.

Tomkins, Calvin. *Duchamp: A Biography.* New York: Henry Holt, 1996.

Twigg, Alan. "John MacKay." *ABCBookWorld.com,* 2004–.

Vinkovetsky, Ilya. *Russian America: An Overseas Colony of a Continental Empire, 1804–1867.* New York: Oxford University Press, 2011.

Virilio, Paul. *War and Cinema: The Logistics of Perception.* Trans. Patrick Camiller. London: Verso, 1989.

Wagner-Martin, Linda. *"Favored Strangers": Gertrude Stein and Her Family.* New Brunswick, NJ: Rutgers University Press, 1995.

Wasserstein, Bernard. *On the Eve: The Jews of Europe before the Second World War.* New York: Simon & Schuster, 2012.

Welch, Stuart Carey. *The Islamic World.* New York: Metropolitan Museum of Art, 2008.

Wright, Robin K., and Daina Augaitis, eds., with Haida advisers Robert Davidson and James Hart. *Charles Edenshaw.* London: Black Dog, 2013.

Colin Browne is the author of *Abraham* (Brick Books, 1987); the critically acclaimed collection of poetry *Ground Water* (Talonbooks, 2002), which was nominated for the Governor General's Literary Award and Dorothy Livesay Poetry Prize; *The Shovel* (Talonbooks, 2007), shortlisted for the 2008 ReLit Award; and *The Properties* (Talonbooks, 2012), nominated for the Dorothy Livesay Poetry Prize. He was an editor of *Writing* magazine and co-founder of the Kootenay School of Writing, Praxis Centre for Screenwriters, and Art of Documentary workshops.

Browne's films include *Linton Garner: I Never Said Goodbye* (2003), *Father and Son* (1992), and *White Lake* (1989), which was nominated for a Genie for Best Feature-Length Documentary. His recent work explores the history and legacy of the Surrealist fascination with the art of the Pacific Northwest coast and Alaska, and includes the catalogue essay "Scavengers of Paradise," published by the Vancouver Art Gallery during its 2011 exhibition, *The Colour of My Dreams: The Surrealism Revolution in Art*. Browne has recently retired from teaching production, screenwriting, and film history at Simon Fraser University's School for the Contemporary Arts.